PRAISE FOR *FEA.*

"Kathryn Haber's *Fear Less, Love More* is life-changing. I could actually feel my cells shifting as I read. I expected to be fed fascinating morsels—and I was—but I hadn't expected to feel bathed in a deep sea of peace, or left with fresh conviction of my great hope: there is a kinder, gentler way to live. Sometimes a book comes along exactly when you need it most. You don't find it; the book finds you. This book was that small miracle for me. It was like having a long conversation with the most wise and loving friend. Honestly, I didn't want it to end."

—Alethea Black, Author of *I Knew You'd Be Lovely* and
You've Been So Lucky Already

"Kathryn has the ability to clearly see the heart of a situation, recreating experiences of great adversity into opportunities for grace and courage. In *Fear Less, Love More*, she shares her hard-earned wisdom while connecting with you like an intimate friend. Her story will inspire you to view your world and connections in a different light. She enables us to lift the veil of fear so we may experience more transcendent love in our lives, reminding us that love and connection is really what life is all about."

—Dr. Lynn Haley, Licensed Psychologist

"I promise you will never look at life's challenges the same way. A deeply personal story sprinkled with actionable truths. A roadmap to hope through the detours of fear, loss and despair. My prayer is that it touches many people as deeply as it touched me."

—Robert Messana, Vice President of Enterprise Sales

"Dr. Kathryn Haber's reminder that we each have one precious life in which to love as much as possible, and that all other endeavors are secondary, is very timely in our current state of weariness. I don't believe it is just a coincidence that she has chosen at this particular time to hold up the starfish as an emblem, one that jogs our memory, and tells us once more that we have more resilience than we know."

—Pam Mayer, PhD, Director, eMindset Academy

Fear Less, Love More: What to Do When the Unexpected Happens
5 Daily Choices

by Dr. Kathryn Haber

© Copyright 2020 Dr. Kathryn Haber

ISBN 978-1-64663-222-0

Published by

köehlerbooks™

3705 Shore Drive
Virginia Beach, VA 23455
800-435-4811
www.koehlerbooks.com

DR. KATHRYN HABER

FEAR LESS, LOVE MORE

What to Do When the Unexpected Happens

5 Daily Choices

VIRGINIA BEACH
CAPE CHARLES

To my dad, mom, sister Debbie, and brother Cal, who passed away from cancer. You were the inspiration for me to share my story, our family story, to help others with their own life challenges. I love and miss you every day.

I *know* our spirits will be together again someday.

TABLE OF CONTENTS

CHOICE #3: CHOOSE PRAYER

CHOICE #4: CHOOSE DIVINE INTERVENTION

CHOICE #5: CHOOSE VULNERABILITY

EPILOGUE

*Permission to use real names has been granted for the majority of the vignettes, and in others where contacts were not made, names have been changed.

1
LIFE HAPPENS

September 2007, Denver, CO

THE PHONE RANG. "KATHRYN, it's Dr. Peters."

"Yes?" I breathed, barely able to get the word out as I juggled Luke, one of our six-month-old twin sons, from one hip to the other.

"I have the pathology results. Turns out they *did* find lymphoma in the node."

I gasped. Then I went silent.

"I'm sorry," he said in a tone too nonchalant for my liking. "Dr. Reece's office will call on Monday. He's an oncologist who specializes in lymphoma. He'll take you through what you need to do for staging, the process of determining if the cancer has spread."

Then he hung up the phone, and my life was forever changed.

✾✾✾

A month prior, I'd felt a lump in my groin about the size of a dime. It didn't hurt, and Dr. Peters, the oncologist I had seen after learning I carried the BRCA1 (breast cancer) gene, assured me it

1

was just an enlarged lymph node. Sure, it *could* be lymphoma, he'd said, but lymphoma patients typically have multiple enlarged nodes and other symptoms, such as night sweats, weight loss, and extreme fatigue—none of which I'd had. Plus, the BRCA1 gene had not been linked to lymphoma, so it was unlikely that this would be the case. He sent me home, suggesting I come back after a month if the node hadn't shrunk.

A month later, it hadn't grown . . . but it hadn't shrunk either. Back I went to Dr. Peters for a needle biopsy. After much angst while waiting on the results, it came back negative. Huge relief . . . or so I thought, until one of Dr. Peters's colleagues filling in for him on the day of my appointment cautioned me that a biopsy might not tell the whole story.

"If I were you," she said, "I'd have the node surgically removed and get the pathology results. It's the only way to be certain it's not cancer."

After some deliberation, my husband, Mark, and I determined it would be best to follow her advice, and I had the node removed entirely so that we would know for sure whether or not it was cancerous.

Which brings us to that phone call on September 15, 2007. "I have the pathology results."

✳✳✳

"I have lymphoma," I said to Mark the moment he walked through the front door of our home in Denver.

He whisked Luke from my hip, kissed him on the forehead, and looked me in the eyes.

"I have cancer," I emphasized, before Mark had a chance to say anything. "Dr. Peters gave me the name of an oncologist who will be setting up tests for staging next week." Tears welled up in my eyes despite my efforts to keep calm.

"Stop it, Kat," Mark said in his empathic but emphatic manner.

"Don't go there. We don't have all the information. It'll be fine. *You,*" he said, looking me in the eyes, "will be fine."

But lymphoma isn't supposed to happen to me, I thought as tears began to fall. I knew I was a BRCA1 gene carrier, so breast and ovarian cancers were on my radar, but lymphoma? It didn't make any sense. And it certainly didn't seem fair.

Back in 2002, I'd heard about the BRCA1 and 2 genes from a Harvard Medical School cancer researcher whom I sat next to on a flight from Boston to Denver. I didn't think the genes pertained to me given we didn't have a lot of cancer in our family history . . . that is, until my sister Debbie was diagnosed in 1998 with breast cancer at the age of forty-three. Simply put, if you have a BRCA mutation, any DNA damage that naturally occurs in your body may not be repaired, which can lead to cancer. According to the National Cancer Institute, for female BRCA carriers, there is a 72 percent chance of getting breast cancer in one's lifetime (as opposed to 12 percent of the general population) and a 44 percent chance of developing ovarian cancer (as opposed to 1.3 percent of the general population). Men can also be BRCA gene carriers. For men with the BRCA gene mutation, there is a 10 percent chance of developing breast cancer in one's lifetime as opposed to 1 percent for the general population. Pancreatic, colon, melanoma and prostate cancers also correlate to the BRCA genes. There is a 50 percent chance of inheriting one of the genes from a parent who has the gene mutation. And even though I didn't know of an extensive history of cancer in my extended family, I had the dreaded gene.

And now I had lymphoma, a cancer seemingly unrelated to the BRCA1 gene.

✻✻✻

Dr. Reece, the oncologist Dr. Peters had referred me to, didn't help matters. In fact, I found him to be quite insensitive. When we were scheduled to meet with him for the first time, Mark stayed home with our boys as our babysitter had a college final to take. This would have typically been a nonissue, as I had no problem going to doctors' appointments by myself. But on this occasion, his absence meant I was left alone for my first meeting with the man who would be telling me my fate.

About 5'7" and round in belly and matching face, he entered the tiny, morgue-cold examination room with a big smile on his face. I sat there in my hospital gown, thinking, *Why is he smiling? I have fucking cancer.*

"This is what you have," he said as he handed me a medical journal article on lymphoma, written by Dr. Arnold S. Freedman from Harvard Medical School and the Dana-Farber Cancer Institute in Boston.

I looked hopelessly from the technical medical jargon in my hand to the doctor standing before me with that smile on his face. "Can you tell me what this all means?" I managed to say.

"Read the article. It's all in there. The good, bad . . . and the ugly," he quipped, finding himself funny, before ushering me to the receptionist to check me out.

How could he be so oblivious to my feelings? I thought. *I'm thirty-eight years old with twin six-month-olds and a three-year-old at home.*

Cancer may have been everyday business for Dr. Reece, but for me it hit home hard. I had lost my father four years prior to pancreatic cancer and my sister Debbie to breast cancer only one year after my dad had passed. Debbie had left two sons behind— Brad, sixteen; and Adam, fourteen. I couldn't bear the thought of leaving my sons behind, too. My anxiety and fear were rampant after the phone call from Dr. Peters.

In the few interactions I had with him, Dr. Reece was all business all the time. In a perpetual rush, he never gave his time and attention to help me process what was happening or ask any questions. His eyes were almost always fixed on my chart, not on me.

Fortunately, I only planned on seeing Dr. Reece for the staging process, which then informs the right course of treatment. Once I knew the stage of my lymphoma, I would be seen by an oncologist in Boston. Originally from Winchester, a suburb eight miles north of Boston, Mark and I planned for the family to move back home for my treatment. I wanted and needed to be close to my mother and brothers during this difficult time. I called my former geneticist oncologist in Boston, Dr. Tasha Nichols at Beth Israel Deaconess Medical Center, and asked her if she would help me find the very best lymphoma doctor in the area.

Dr. Nichols got back to me immediately with the name Dr. Arnie Freedman, the very same oncologist who authored the article Dr. Reece had given me on my first visit with him.

When I told Dr. Reece I was planning on being treated in Boston and that I had an initial consultation set up with Dr. Freedman, his curiosity was piqued for the first time since I'd met him. He seemed more interested in working with Freedman through my transition than in handling my staging.

It can take weeks to determine exactly what stage you are, depending on when you get in for testing and how quickly the scans can be read, and of course all you can imagine is your cancer spreading as time passes. And despite my efforts to schedule my staging process sooner versus later, Dr. Reece lacked a sense of urgency.

I dissolved into tears with the scheduler. "If you could please find me a time to get in for staging this week, I'd greatly appreciate it," I managed to say. Crying in front of strangers wasn't my modus operandi. I was typically a bit more put together. The scheduler looked me in the eyes, got up from behind her desk, and gave me an empathic hug, *and* her next available appointment—my first inkling that showing vulnerability perhaps wasn't such a bad thing.

❋❋❋

The morning of my positron emission tomography (PET) scan that would determine my stage of cancer, one of my dear friends, Jill, happened to knock on my door.

Jill lived in Colorado Springs, about seventy miles from us. At the time, she had three-year-old twins and an eight-year-old—all of whom were with her. Jill was never "just in the neighborhood," and I hadn't yet told her about my cancer. In fact, I had told virtually no one about my cancer at that point. The thought of others pitying me—the woman who had lost her father and sister to cancer, and now was diagnosed with cancer too, with six-month-old twins and a three-year-old at home—was too much for me to bear.

The second I opened the door and saw her beaming face, I dissolved into tears and told her everything. She canceled her day's plans and went to the PET scan with me, all of her kids in tow. They don't make friends better than that, one of many silver linings during this experience.

Ten days later, the phone rang again.

"Kathryn, I have your staging results," said Dr. Reece's nurse cheerfully.

Really, I thought, *he couldn't call me himself?*

"OK," I said. "And . . . "

"According to the PET scan, you have been diagnosed with stage I follicular non-Hodgkin's lymphoma, grade 3. It has a 93 percent cure rate."

I sighed with relief. I'd taken the phone call in the parking lot of a client's office in San Francisco, too secretive about my illness to take the call inside, within earshot of my client. I was doing my very best to compartmentalize work and health. I had told a few select friends about my illness, but certainly not my clients.

"Can you tell me what grade 3 means?" I asked her. I knew that stage I meant that the cancer had been found in only one group of lymph nodes, in my case my inguinal gland.

"I'm not exactly sure what grade 3 means. Why don't you Google it and get all the details?" she said in all seriousness.

Really? I thought. *She's telling me to "Google it"?*

Exasperated, I managed *goodbye* and hung up the phone. At least I now knew the stage of the cancer and could start focusing on getting back to Boston to be cared for by Dr. Freedman and the Dana Farber Cancer Institute team. I got back on the phone and started making plans for my family and me to move back East.

A clinical psychologist by education, I had decided in the last year of my doctoral program that I wanted to blend business and psychology and enter the field of organizational psychology. After graduation, I spent ten years at Somerville Partners, a boutique organizational consulting firm in Denver, learning the art and science of business psychology. Founder Kevin Somerville took me under his wing and became my mentor. Over ten years, he taught me everything I needed to know to do the work effectively. I'm forever grateful to him.

Being a consultant, I was accustomed to flying to my clients wherever they were located, and doing so from Boston would be just as easy as it was from Denver.

So, Mark and I and our three young boys left Denver in October 2007, one month after diagnosis, and rented a home on the northeast seaboard in Newburyport, Massachusetts. I flew out first with our twins, Jake and Luke, who were then seven months old. Mark stayed behind for a couple of weeks with Harry, our three-year-old, who had the croup and was contagious and unable to fly.

When we got to Newburyport, I called Diane, my first friend in life and next-door neighbor growing up, and asked her to go with me to my first chemotherapy appointment, scheduled for the day before Halloween. A determined working mother of three and busier than most, Diane dropped everything to be with me.

"I want to be 'your person,' Kit," she said, using my childhood nickname. "I'm here for you." Another silver lining.

And there we were . . . I sat in a recliner in the chemotherapy infusion room, waiting for my first five-hour infusion of the cocktail CHOP-R: Cytoxan, hydroxyrubicin, Oncovin, prednisone, and rituximab—the chemotherapy drugs designed to kill my cancer without killing me. Diane sat in an office-like chair next to me trying her best to distract me with stories from *People* magazine and the latest styles from *Vogue*.

I couldn't help but think of my sister Debbie. Just three years prior, she'd sat in a similar recliner, and her chemo had ultimately failed to keep her alive. I watched her pass away before her fiftieth birthday. *We lost her so young,* I thought as I waited, *and now here I am with my own cancer fight ahead of me . . . and I'm only thirty-eight years old. Will I have the same fate?* Although I was stage I and had a 93 percent survival probability, given that I'd lost my dad and sister, I felt nothing but fear, not having my faith or any of the coping tools I have today.

Then I saw Janine, Debbie's oncology nurse. We locked eyes and she darted over to me from across the room. I'd gotten to know Janine during the years of Debbie's breast cancer treatment. She was compassionate, knowledgeable, and had a great sense of humor. And she just adored my sister, which always filled my heart with joy, especially when Debbie was suffering through tough treatments.

"Kit! What are you doing here?" she asked with her thick Boston accent.

"I was diagnosed with lymphoma last month," I said, my eyes

again welling with tears. Janine's eyes welled too, the memory of my sister's last days written on her face. "Don't worry," I said. "Arnie Freedman is my oncologist. I'm stage I. Stage I," I repeated, to reassure myself as much as to reassure her, not truly believing my own words.

I wanted to say, *I have fucking cancer. I have three baby boys at home. Please don't let me die. I can't have the same fate as my father and sister.*

She sighed with relief.

"Kit, that *is* great news—an excellent prognosis," she said, sitting next to me in the same type of chair I'd spent so many hours sitting in when I was with Debbie and now Diane was sitting in—being my person. "I don't believe in coincidence. I was just transferred here to the hematology floor from the breast cancer floor. I was meant to be here with you today."

I looked around the busy infusion room, a big, open space full of recliners flanked by two chairs for the "special someones" accompanying their loved one dealing with the Big C. There were at least twenty other patients. Each of us had our own recliner; each of us had our own unique story. And though we were bound together in a collective fight against our cancer, though we were dealing with our own misfortunes the mood was oddly . . . positive. Here we were, some bald heads, some scarf-covered, face masks, rolling IVs with cocktails flowing through our veins, ready to rally around one another. We were all part of a community hell-bent on beating the odds.

❀❀❀

Thankfully, Mark was able to join me for my second of three infusions, which I had every three weeks. It felt good to have my husband to lean on—I rarely leaned on anyone, priding myself on my strong independence I developed in my young-adult years; showing vulnerability was not my thing. But now,

I desperately needed support, being faced with a challenge that felt larger than life.

I was sitting in my recliner next to a man probably in his mid-fifties. His wife, approximately ten years his junior, was by his side. She was energetic with a stylistic flair and exuded an air of optimism.

"Hi, I'm Jim." The man reached to shake my hand. "And this is my wife, Lynn. What brings you here?" he said, chuckling.

"Lymphoma. Follicular," I said with my best smile. "Stage I, but grade 3 . . . which apparently is an aggressive form. I have three rounds of CHOP-R, then radiation. You?"

"I'm one of the lucky ones," he said sarcastically. "This is my second bout with cancer. First time was five years ago. Bladder. Now it's leukemia. stage IV."

What! Second bout, Stage IV? Yet Jim and his wife, Lynn, were so warm and seemed in good spirits despite it all.

"This is your second round of chemo?" Lynn asked.

I nodded. "I guess my hair will be falling out soon . . ."

"Get your hair cut short first," Lynn said matter-of-factly, "and then shave it once you notice it falling out."

"It makes it less . . . you know . . . traumatizing," Jim said with a wink and a smile.

This was hard to digest, but I knew it would happen. My thick, long brown hair, which had always been part of my feminine identity, would soon be gone. Who would I be after that?

Lynn shook me from my reverie. "I'm off to grab some coffee at Dunkin's. What can I get the both of you?"

"No thanks, all set," Mark and I said in unison.

Lynn returned thirty minutes later, about halfway through my five-hour infusion. The slow drip of the drugs into my veins had to be exact; it was a process that could not be rushed. At times, I would feel a cooling sensation and at others a warming one, depending on the type of toxin dribbling into my veins. I tried to keep my mind off the fact that poisons were entering my body, and instead visualized the drugs killing my cancer cells.

Lynn handed me a Target bag. Inside, I found a bright-red electric hair shaver, something similar to what you see at hair salons.

"I thought you could use this."

I was so taken aback by the warmth and kindness of complete strangers that I began to cry. We exchanged phone numbers and addresses. Mark used that shaver on me one week later, shaving my head Thanksgiving morning. Six months after that, we received a card from Lynn in the mail. Jim had died.

THANK YOU, NURSE

We all know cancer doesn't discriminate. It is devastating, no matter who you are, what your profession is, or how "good" you try to live your life. *Life* happens; it too does not discriminate—it keeps happening. Given my BRCA1 diagnosis, six months after my chemo and radiation for lymphoma, at thirty-nine years old, I had my ovaries removed and a prophylactic double mastectomy and reconstruction of my breasts. The removal of my breasts perhaps should have been more traumatic than it was. My breasts were relatively small to begin with and, after breastfeeding three babies, less than taut. So, the idea of a new set was actually okay with me. I didn't truly have a choice given the dreary statistic of a 72 percent chance of breast cancer in my lifetime if I chose not to remove them. What I remember most about that surgery was the well-seasoned nurse who checked me in. She was reviewing my history and didn't hold back her disbelief about my "bad luck."

"Four miscarriages, your father died four years ago, your sister three years ago, you went through chemo and radiation for lymphoma last year, you had an oophorectomy earlier this year and now you're having your breasts removed? Really? I've never seen someone with such a bad history." *Thank you, nurse.* Just what I wanted to hear before heading into surgery.

❋❋❋

IMPERFECTION AND POSITIVITY

We are human and, by definition, imperfect. We live our lives in imperfect ways, trying our best to make it through each day. Each of us has our own unique life stories, our joys, our challenges—and certainly our fears. While fear is part of the natural human condition, if we submit to it, we're in jeopardy of recoiling from life, isolating ourselves, and staying exactly where—and who—we are, not growing into the people we are born to be in this life.

Seven years after my cancer fight, I lost my brother Cal to pancreatic cancer and my mother the following year of the same devastating disease. Through these losses and other challenging life experiences, I have learned that we must courageously push through our fears, if we want to deepen our characters and our understanding of what it means to be human—and ultimately live a fulfilled life. Although I have a heightened genetic risk of cancer recurrence being BRCA1 positive, I refuse to live this life in a constant state of fear. Instead, I think positively about my health, knowing that positivity and optimism have been empirically proven to have a positive impact on health. And I am vigilant with my cancer screenings: Every year I have an endoscopic ultrasound (EUS) and an MRI/MRCP of my pancreas to determine if I have pancreatic cancer. Every year I have my skin checked for melanoma and every three years, I have a colonoscopy to check for colon cancer. I have blood tests every three to six months to check for any changes in my white blood counts and certain tumor markers. I know—it's a lot of testing. Every time I feel an ache or a pain, I could think, *Is it cancer?*

But I don't. I *choose* not to. Instead, I choose to trust that I will be okay, even if I die (more on this later).

Rather than make it through each day, I learned how to thrive, not just survive, through life's challenges—to feel at peace, with a sense of purpose and fulfillment. I felt a calling, if you will, to share my revelations with others through these pages.

Most of us experience difficult life challenges at some point. Mine come mostly from cancer; yours may come from something different—perhaps the passing of a loved one, the sickness of a parent, a debilitating accident, living with chronic disease, physical or emotional abuse, addiction, divorce, mental illness . . . unfortunately, the list goes on. Whatever your challenge, I hope you find some solace here.

In this book, I will share five *interrelated* choices you can courageously make every day, every moment, to live a more fulfilling, centered life, no matter what challenge you face. When the unexpected happens, you *always* have the opportunity to *choose* how you will respond. I have included some reflection exercises with some questions to answer or thoughts to consider to help you integrate the five choices into your everyday life. I recommend having a journal or notebook handy to capture your thoughts and feelings.

❋❋❋

IT'S NOT ALL ABOUT ME

Before my lymphoma diagnosis, I was an agnostic. I was raised Protestant but neither believed nor disbelieved in God or life after death. I went to church on Sundays because my mother didn't give my siblings and me a choice, but I didn't give faith much thought. Today, coming to faith—the belief that there is something beyond myself and this earthly existence—has been the most important experience of my life. When diagnosed with cancer, I finally realized and accepted that I wasn't in control of whether I lived or died. The only thing I could do was hand over my life to a higher power and do my best to be vigilant with my prophylactic surgeries and screenings to stay alive and be here to raise my children and provide support and guidance to others along the way.

For me, God is what I found and what got me through. For you, it could be the Universe, Buddha, Allah, Love, the Divine, Shiva, the Source, etc. If this is too hard for you to fathom, start with believing in something beyond yourself; it may be as simple as believing in your community. In fact, Archbishop Desmond Tutu describes finding happiness through the support of his community even in the midst of fighting prostate cancer. In the Dalai Lama and Desmond Tutu's book, *The Book of Joy*, Tutu shares, "One of the good things is realizing that you are not a solitary cell. You are part of a wonderful community. You open, you blossom, really because of other people" (2016, 43).

Human beings are biologically wired to be in connection with each other—to love ourselves and our neighbor. The neuropsychology and heart psychology are clear on this. We have neurons in our brains that emit the feel-good chemicals dopamine and serotonin, *and* we have neurons around the right ventricles of our hearts, which researchers refer to as the "heart brain." These neurons emit the "cuddle" hormone, oxytocin. These neurotransmitters create a sense of joy and happiness within us that others can *feel* and mirror. When we think beyond ourselves and give to others we are physically and emotionally creating a peacefulness in our bodies and souls and a fulfillment that we cannot experience when we live in isolation.

If we choose to move beyond a faith in our community toward a belief that there is more to this life than the day-to-day challenging earthly existence—that there is a joyous, loving, divine state—we can take the pressure off ourselves to be "perfect" in this life. Why strive for something that can't be attained? We will only find disappointment at the end of each and every day. Why do that to ourselves? Brené Brown, social worker, *New York Times* best-selling author, and a research professor at the University of Houston, shares in her book *Daring Greatly* that each day we must tell ourselves, "No matter what gets done and how much is left undone, I am enough" (2015, 10).

Once we *choose* to have faith in something beyond ourselves, our fears begin to melt away, and we can become more centered with the universe, because we realize we are not the center of the universe. This, at least, was the case for me, and for many people who have survived a number of hard challenges in their lives. If we have faith things will work out, if we believe, if we *know* that no matter what happens, everything will be okay—even in death, as our souls live on—we won't "sweat the small stuff" as much. For me, having the courage to put my trust in the universe that things will work out as they should puts life in perspective, mitigating fears and anxieties. *Courage*, a word that comes from the Latin word *cor*, meaning "heart," is what we need to push through our fears. Suddenly, taking that promotion at work feels more manageable, or that presentation that you are giving to 500 people doesn't feel as daunting. What we may have feared in the past no longer feels as scary. It's a releasing and miraculous experience when we let go of our fears. Of course, acquiring this deep faith didn't just happen overnight. It was a tumultuous journey.

✻✻✻

TUMULT

My lymphoma diagnosis in 2007 shook me to my core. I was fearful and depressed. The loss of control over whether I would live or die left me feeling vulnerable. I was scared for my family. The thought of not being around to raise my boys was almost too much to bear; it left me raw. All these fears on the heels of losing my sister and my father . . . I wasn't sure how to keep it together emotionally or physically.

I realized I didn't have an ounce of control. This was the hardest part for me. I could not cure my cancer. For the first time in my life, it seemed, the outcome wasn't up to me. I thought I had made my own way in life. I was a psychologist and a financially independent woman. I believed I created my own destiny and used to think I could solve any problem or challenge thrown my way. But this? I couldn't fix this no matter how hard I tried.

A disease that had already taken so much from me now threatened to take my life; it was uncharted territory. My strong sense of independence disintegrated the moment I got that call from Dr. Peters. What's worse, I kept it all inside. The thought of being pitied by others kept me from sharing my plight with most. I did not have the courage to show my vulnerability. I rebuffed the thought of opening myself up to any love and support outside my husband and a few close friends and family members. The pain, fear, anger, anxiety, and sadness churned inside me. I continued to work full time as an organizational psychologist and *act* strong, despite the tumult in my body and soul.

❊❊❊

FINDING FAITH ON THE BATHROOM FLOOR

A few weeks after my diagnosis, I hit rock bottom. My heart raced. My head spun. I felt a deep sense of panic. I stumbled to the bathroom, where I collapsed onto the floor, utterly spent. All I could think about were my boys.

What would happen to them if I died? How would they manage in this world without their mother? What would Mark do? Would he remarry? Would the boys have a stepmother? On and on and on the thoughts raced, and my heart rate spiked.

What happened next is still hard to believe.

Kneeling on the cold bathroom floor, tears streaking my cheeks, out of nowhere, I started to pray.

"God," I said, "please help me. If you exist, please help me. I need you. I'm so scared."

"God," I pled, "I *can't* die. My babies need their mother. I need them. Mark can't possibly raise them all on his own. *Please* give me strength. *Please* help me through this. *Please* . . . let me live. I am only thirty-eight. I want more time. I have so much more to give. *Please* give me the strength to survive."

Prayer hadn't been my thing. I had never prayed as an adult, and only prayed the Lord's Prayer as a child. So, this was quite unusual for me. The only reason I started speaking to God that day on the bathroom floor was because I was at my wit's end; it felt like my last resort.

After pleading, praying, and crying for about ten minutes, I started to feel . . . *different.* I suddenly felt *lighter.* It was as if my anguish was melting away. My heart rate slowed. My breathing relaxed. The images of my sons without their mother subsided. I felt . . . a *release.*

Is this possible? I asked myself. *Has God answered my prayers? Could there* be *a God?*

2

Choice #1: Choose FAITH

ANSWERED PRAYERS?

ALBERT EINSTEIN, THEORETICAL PHYSICIST
and founder of modern physics, recognized the impossibility
of a universe created without a higher spirit. According to
Max Jammer's *Einstein and Religion: Physics and Theology*,
Einstein is quoted as saying, "Everyone who is seriously
committed to the cultivation of science becomes convinced that
in all the laws of the universe is manifest a spirit vastly superior
to man, and to which we with our powers must feel humble"
(2002).

Charles Darwin, evolutionary biologist, naturalist, and
geologist, believed in God as the creator of the universe. He, too,
believed in the relationship between science and faith. In his
book *Descent of Man*, Darwin states, "The theory of evolution is
fully compatible with faith in God. I think the greatest argument
for the existence in God is the impossibility of demonstrating
and understanding that the immense universe, sublime above all
measure, and man were the result of chance" (2004). And in *The*

Book of Joy, Archbishop Tutu and the Dalai Lama claim, "Too often we see spirituality and science as antagonistic forces, each with its hand at the other's throat" (2016, 5). They go on to say that in actuality many different fields of science come to the same conclusion that there is something beyond our physical reality.

When I read these greats after my experience on the bathroom floor, they deeply resonated with me. That next morning, after praying, I felt a peace I hadn't experienced since my diagnosis. It felt *miraculous*.

Is this for real? I asked myself. *Can it really be* this *easy?*

The prayer my panic induced had eased my heart, but had I really "spoken" to God? Had God actually answered my prayers, or had I managed to get myself out of my state of panic? The psychologist in me wanted to claim the latter, but I *knew* it was something more. I had felt a power beyond my physical reality. I had a sense of *knowing* deep in my core.

From that day on the bathroom floor forward, I decided to start attending church and become a student of faith.

❈❈❈❈

ONE AND DONE?

While I prayed to a Christian god, that does not have to be your god or faith. What matters is that you believe in a power beyond yourself. Wherever you read "God," feel free to substitute your higher power, your divine.

Rick Warren says in his book *The Purpose Driven Life*, "The most profound and intimate experiences of worship will likely be in your darkest days when you turn to God alone" (2002).

For me, he's right. Many people say that when they are first diagnosed with the Big C, they have a demarcation in their lives: life *before* diagnosis and life *after* diagnosis.

This is true for me as well. I have lived two lives: the one *before* that phone call from Dr. Peters, and the one full of faith and love and fulfillment *after* that call. And all from cancer. Who knew?

I was sharing my spiritual journey with my good friend and colleague Mawi Asgedom, author of *Of Beetles and Angels* and one of Oprah's most influential people, when he asked if I had read any works by Marianne Williamson. To him, much of what I was describing sounded similar to Williamson's journey. I hadn't heard of her at the time and made a note to check her out.

Interestingly, or as divine intervention would have it, that very next morning I received an email from the Shift Network, an education company whose members aspire to create a sustainable, prosperous, and peaceful world. They were featuring Marianne Williamson as their keynote speaker in their webinar series. I logged onto the series and heard Williamson for the first time.

Listening to Williamson speak about finding love and peace in the world by releasing fear and believing in a spiritual power beyond our day-to-day existence on earth was very powerful. Her words deeply resonated with me, as I was experiencing the same phenomenon.

After that encounter with Williamson, I read several of her books, my favorite being *A Return to Love*. She writes,

> My fear finally became so great, that I wasn't too hip to say, "God, please help me." . . . As painful as this experience was, I now see it as an important, perhaps necessary step in my breakthrough to a happier life . . . . God rescues those whose spirit is dim and awakens it with the light of the Holy Spirit. (1992, 10, 12)

I feel the same way. Though it has not been an easy journey, I feel blessed to have found faith when I did. Life's challenges don't stop coming. A friend of mine once said nothing else bad could happen to her after she was diagnosed with breast cancer.

I couldn't disagree more. I wish life worked that way—one and done—but it doesn't. My life is much more peaceful and fulfilling since I found my spiritual core, but it isn't because nothing worse than cancer can come along to challenge me.

Because I have faith—in myself, in my community, in God, in the goodness of the universe, that my soul will continue to live, even after death—I believe I can handle the unexpected that comes my way.

REFLECT

Answer the following in your journal:
- If you have a faith, describe what it is.
- Do you believe in an existence that extends beyond you? Beyond your community? Beyond this life? Why or why not?

❁❁❁

CONTROL ISSUES?

As mentioned, my cancer diagnosis led me to the realization that I had *no* control of whether I lived or died. I only had control of how I *responded* to it, and it took an epiphany on the bathroom floor to accept this and give myself over to a higher power. When we *choose* to have faith and let go of control, we can see that our salvation lies in that higher power, a power beyond ourselves.

Marianne Williamson in *A Return to Love* shares the following:

> For many people, things have to get very bad before there's a shift. When you truly bottom out, there comes an exhilarating release. You recognize there is power in the universe bigger than you are, who can do for you what you can't do for yourself. All of a sudden, your last resort sounds like a very good idea. (1992, 13)

I indeed was powerless, and, unwittingly, I put everything in the divine's hands. And my fears began to disintegrate.

REFLECT

Answer the following in your journal:

- Describe a time when you tried to control a situation or person. What were the outcomes? How did it make you feel?
- Describe a time when you gave up control of a situation or person. What were the outcomes? How did it make you feel?
- What one thing can you commit to relinquishing control over this week?

❀❀❀

DESPERATION IS NOT A REQUIREMENT

Recently at church, up at the pulpit, a member of our congregation shared his faith story. He had been living what others might describe as "the good life." He had plenty of money, a sports car, a boat, a beautiful home on the ocean, a lovely wife, and a baby on the way.

Despite all of this, Steve felt empty inside. He was drinking and drugging too much and was, as he described, "at the end of himself." He had hit *his* rock bottom and was planning a way to take his life when, anguished in bed, he called out, "God, if you are real, I need to know now. Please give me a sign, give me strength, help me to survive. I need you, God." My body trembled while listening to him in the sanctuary, as his story was eerily similar to my own.

Almost immediately his heart filled with love, his pain melted away, and he *felt* the words "I am." He, too, was in disbelief of this powerful, life-altering experience, and it was the beginning of *his* spiritual journey.

When I heard Steve's story and reflected on my own—and

the many others I'd heard in my time since my journey toward faith—I couldn't help but wonder, *Do we have to be in a crisis, at the "end of ourselves," on our knees, at rock bottom to find faith?*

I met with my pastor to ask him this very question.

Like Williamson, Warren, and me, Pastor Jeff said many people find faith when they've hit rock bottom, but he also assured me that there are many people who find faith without tragedy, himself included. He'd attended church his entire life but never considered being a pastor until, in his thirties, he felt a *calling* to follow Christ.

"You just woke up one day and felt . . . a calling?" I asked incredulously.

"Well, not exactly," he said with a smile. "I was enjoying my career as a technical engineer, *and* I'd always cared deeply for Christ, so it wasn't completely out of the blue."

After thoughtful discussions with his family, he decided to go to seminary and become a pastor. The "calling" was a sensation he just couldn't say no to, a divine invitation without a single tragedy in his life. He went on to share many stories of those who have deep faith without hitting rock bottom first.

It was reassuring to hear that you don't have to wait to be at the end of yourself, desperate, to find faith in something beyond yourself. God doesn't *want* you to hit rock bottom. The divine just wants to draw you near. No matter how faith comes to you, *choose* to believe in a power beyond yourself, and see where it takes you.

�֍�֍✖

OUR SOULS LIVE ON

I've experienced great loss in my life and know with my BRCA1 gene that my future is uncertain, yet I am not fearful of death. I could see BRCA1 as a ticking time bomb, but I don't. I have an intuitive sense that God wants me to be a vessel for his Word and work. I believe He wants me on earth to support and guide others on their journeys. And if this is not the case, then death means going home to be with my father, mother, brother, and sister, and those who have passed on to the spiritual realm of the divine.

Horrific things happen in this world minute to minute. Murder, rape, suicide, war, famine, natural disasters, political and civic unrest, pandemics . . . unfortunately, the list goes on. And yet, there are countless silver linings that also emerge in times of tragedy, showing the divine's love and work. This life is temporal. Choose to believe that our souls live on; it is a *choice*. Any of us can die at any moment. Try to let go of the fear of dying and recognize that death is not the worst thing that can happen, as the eternal is a loving, joyous state without the pain and suffering of this world. If this is too difficult to fathom right away, consider how the Dalai Lama and Archbishop Tutu square life's tragedies in *The Book of Joy*:

> Yes, we do have setbacks [in the world], but you must keep everything in perspective. The world is getting better. Think about the rights of women or how slavery was considered morally justified a few hundred years ago. It takes time. We are growing and learning how to be compassionate, how to be caring, how to be human. (2016, 117)

❋❋❋

PAST-LIFE REGRESSION

A few years ago, a good friend of mine from graduate school, Lee, asked if I would be one of his "subjects" for a past-life regression hypnosis session. Past-life regression is a technique that uses hypnosis to help patients uncover memories of past lives or incarnations.

Lee had recently had a profound experience with Dr. Linda Backman, a renowned past-life regressionist, and decided to pursue past-life regression further, this time as a therapist rather than as a patient.

In order to get certified in past-life regression, he needed to practice on people who were open to the idea. I was very excited to participate. I had read *Many Lives, Many Masters* by Brian Weiss, MD, and was intrigued by the concept of past lives. Through reading about Weiss's life-altering experiences unlocking past lives of many of his patients, which in turn freed them from their fears, I was beyond eager to have my own profound experience that day with my trusted friend.

I lay down on Lee's brown leather couch in his finished basement in Central Park, our mutual neighborhood. I was wrapped in a wool blanket; my head rested on a red throw pillow. The lights were dim. I was feeling relaxed and comfortable. Lee spoke in a calm, measured way, taking me through his script to get me into a trance-like state.

Shortly, I was hypnotized. My limbs were heavy. My breathing had a rhythmic cadence. When Lee asked me how I was feeling, my voice was monotone and without affect. Although in a trance, when it came to doors to previous lives, unfortunately they were disappointingly empty.

Lee had me travel down virtual staircases and stand in front of potential doors on the precipices of past lives, but every door I opened led nowhere. No matter what staircases he had me walk down and what sort of door I came to, I found no past lives.

After about thirty minutes of his gallant efforts, Lee asked, "Kathryn, shall I take you out of your trance?"

"No," I said. Then to my surprise, I added, "I'd like to connect with my sister Debbie."

Lee was not prepared for this. Nor was I. We hadn't discussed any such desire in advance of the session, but the moment I said my sister's name, a vibrant, almost psychedelic red light *enveloped* me; the light and energy felt like it was hovering over my entire body. Tears spilled from my eyes, and my smile grew broad.

"Kathryn, what's happening right now?" Lee asked in his measured, calm way, yet his voice seemed distant, as if he were at the end of a tunnel. I didn't respond, not wanting the light to fade away by talking to him.

It was Debbie. There was no question. I *felt* her speak even if I didn't hear any words. She *imprinted* on my soul. There were no words or pictures that I heard or saw. It was just a *knowing*.

I *felt* the words, "Cal is going to be just fine." Our brother Cal was battling pancreatic cancer at the time. The moment I felt that, I *knew* he was going to pass away and that he was going to be in a loving, joyous, spiritual place, with her, our father, and the divine.

My sister went on.

"You are meant to be on this earth," she imprinted on my soul. "BRCA1 will not be your end. You are meant to make a difference in this world."

She then drifted away, and Lee brought me out of my hypnotic state.

When I told Lee everything that had happened in the trance, he could hardly believe it. We were both overcome with emotion. I had heard of people who had near-death experiences and spoke about communication in the afterlife being a *knowing* or an *imprint*, but I didn't truly understand what this meant until I experienced it myself.

Hours later, when Lee's wife returned home, she said to Lee, "How did the session go with Kathryn? When I walked into the house I felt this energy that was . . . *enveloping*." Exactly how I felt as the psychedelic red light came over me. She used the *same* word.

✲✲✲

FAITH IN THE STAIRCASE

I was blessed to connect with Debbie's spirit, as it validated my growing faith and allowed me to share this experience with Cal before he passed away, reassuring him that there is, indeed, a possibility of an afterlife. This meant a lot to him. As Martin Luther King Jr. said, "Faith is taking the first step even when you don't see the whole staircase."

I now have faith that life will work out as it should, and as a result, I feel more grounded and centered. Take writing this book. I heard time and time again that it is extremely difficult these days to find a publisher willing to publish a manuscript from an unknown author, which is why so many people choose the self-publishing route. Although hearing this from many, I *knew* I would find a publisher; I had faith that I would ultimately find one. "All it takes is one," I would say to Mark, after receiving *many* "no thank-yous" to my *many* query letters. And then, one Sunday morning, I received an email from John Koehler, saying one of his persnickety editors read my work and gave it a thumbs-up. *All it takes is one*, and *faith* that it will happen.

For the years I have been writing this book, I envisioned that it would ultimately come to fruition. Visualization is a very powerful tool that is also substantiated by brain research. If you can *see*, *taste*, and *feel* your end state, the neurons in your brain interpret the visualization as similar to real-life experience—creating new neural pathways that prime us to act in accordance to what we visualized—without actually physically doing anything. How cool is that? Practice visualization and never lose *faith in the staircase*.

❋❋❋

AMAZING GRACE

A few years ago, while at church, our pastor asked us to open the hymn book to "Amazing Grace," a hymn I have sung many times in my life. I did as instructed, but this time, as I sang (terribly, I might add), I felt deep emotion.

> Amazing grace, how sweet the sound
> that saved a wretch like me.
> I once was lost, but now am found,
> Was blind, but now I see.
> 'Twas grace that taught my heart to fear,
> and grace my fears relieved.
> How precious did that grace appear
> the hour I first believed.

Next thing I knew, I was crying tears of joy. "Amazing Grace" described *exactly* what had happened to me on the bathroom floor and in the years that followed. I was once lost; now I was found. I was blind and now I could see. I just let the music *envelop* me, I let the tears fall, and I let the words deepen my faith.

❋❋❋

*"When we meet tragedy in life, we can react in two ways—
either by losing hope and falling into self-destructive habits,
or by using the challenge to find our inner strength."*
The Fourteenth Dalai Lama

Choose to have faith that operating from a place of love allows us to move through our fears and meet every day's challenges, however large or small. Choose to believe we are part of a greater existence, and we will feel more peaceful and centered in life.

Peace is an internal state, not one that comes from external pleasures such as seeing a good movie or going to an amusement park or receiving a thoughtful gift from a friend. Peace is deeper than happiness; it's how we feel at our spiritual core. It's a neurobiological fact that when we give and express compassion toward others we experience peace and greater fulfillment. Health psychologist Kelly McGonigal researched the effects of oxytocin in our bodies, or the "cuddle" hormone I referred to earlier:

> Oxytocin primes you to do things that strengthen close relationships. It makes you crave physical contact with your friends and family. It enhances your empathy. It even makes you more willing to help and support the people you care about. (2013)

It's certainly been the case for me on my faith journey, and has been a powerful, integral part of feeling at peace and fulfilled in life. But this wasn't always the case.

3

Choice #2: Choose LOVE

EGOCENTRIC VS. ECO-CENTRIC?

WHEN WE OPERATE FROM a place of fear, we operate *ego*centrically and behave in unproductive ways. When we are fearful, we go into "fight, flight, or freeze" mode and feel the need to protect ourselves. In fight or flight, it is perfectly normal to find our hearts racing, our skin flushed, our pupils dilated, or our bodies trembling—or, in the case of "freeze," our parasympathetic system dominates and we freeze, or in severe cases faint. Back in the days of our ancestors, this cortisol and adrenaline rush helped us survive against dangerous threats— e.g., lions, tigers, and bears. But today, even *perceived* threats can make our central nervous system go haywire. Psychologically speaking, in the face of fear we start to protect ourselves with "me" or ego behaviors—like feeling the need to control, shutting others out, playing the victim, being reactive, passive-aggressive, manipulative, etc. We put ourselves before the collective good or the community because we feel we are in real or perceived danger and therefore we think and behave egocentrically.

We human beings are great at beating ourselves up. We tell ourselves we aren't good enough, thin enough, funny enough, attractive enough, smart enough, etc. However, when we replace this negative self-talk with positive self-talk that is loving—we are good enough, we have gifts and talents that are valued, we are loved, we are worthy of love—and have faith that "we've got this," the relief we can experience is incredibly powerful. When we are good to ourselves, when we know we are worthy of love and love ourselves, then we can give of ourselves to others.

When we show compassion and care toward others, we are operating from love, not fear. When we operate from a place of love, we are no longer egocentric, but rather, we are eco-centric, looking to improve the whole—our entire ecosystem, the environment, our community, the universe. When we trust in ourselves, each other, the universe, we are our best selves. We are more caring, compassionate, and gracious toward others, and we are less judgmental or short-tempered and more patient and respectful. This choice of love gives us a sense of purpose in this life and yields great fulfillment, knowing we are helping others and living the life we were born to live.

In *A Return to Love*, Williamson says it best:

> Love is what we were born with. Fear is what we have learned here. The spiritual journey is the relinquishment— or unlearning—of fear and the acceptance of love back into our hearts . . . . It is our ultimate reality and our purpose on earth . . . . To experience love in ourselves and others, is the meaning of life. (1992, xxii)

When we are acting in a loving, eco-centric way, the universe more often than not brings that love and compassion back to us. Positive energy flows, and things work out in positive ways. Conversely, when we live in fear and behave egocentrically, we find ourselves "stuck" in our negative self-talk, and in victim mode, finding it hard to move forward with hope and optimism.

REFLECT

Answer the following in your journal:

- When have you operated in an egocentric way? What did your behaviors look like? What was the outcome?
- When have you operated in an eco-centric way? What did your behaviors look like? What was the outcome?
- Compare those two experiences. Which worked out better for you?
- What one eco-centric behavior can you commit to this week?

❊❊❊

PUT YOUR OXYGEN MASK ON FIRST

In order to love in eco-centric ways, we must love ourselves first. We must put on our own oxygen mask before trying to help others. This means getting back to basics with eating healthy, exercising, and sleeping well. Of course, every individual is unique; it's always wise to check in with your health professional to learn what's best for you.

Eating small, nutritious meals/snacks about every three hours helps with our metabolism and evens out our blood sugar levels. If possible, have your largest meal of the day be lunch, not dinner, as our bodies are primed to digest midday, not in the evenings. It's best to minimize sugar and processed foods, too.

In addition, salmon, oysters, anchovies, flax, and chia seeds are high in omega 3—the single best nutrient for the brain—and blueberries, almonds, and dark chocolate are rich in antioxidants, which help to fight against free radicals that can compromise our immune systems. Drinking plenty of water, striving for eight 8-ounce glasses per day, increases our metabolism, keeps us hydrated, flushes out toxins, regulates body temperature, aids in digestion, and even makes us smarter. *Who can argue with that?*

As well as taking good care of ourselves from a nutrition standpoint, try to add in at least thirty minutes of exercise three to five times a week, mixed with some weight training for best results. Getting at least six hours of sleep each night also helps us show up as our best selves each day. And remember it's important to be kind to ourselves. We human beings are not perfect, so when we indulge in something that may not be the healthiest, or miss a couple of exercise routines, let's be gentle with ourselves. Get back on track the next day, rather than slip off track for too long. When we show ourselves compassion, we are then able to show compassion and care for others.

REFLECT

- What act of self-care can you commit to today? Eating healthier? Exercising more? Getting more sleep?
- Try not to overreach with your goals. Start off with small changes that you can achieve. Then slowly add to your goals. If you fall off track, be gentle with yourself and begin again.

❊❊❊

BASEMENT OR BALCONY?

Keynote inspirational speaker Dr. Adolph Brown believes there are "balcony" people and "basement" people. Balcony people see the glass as half full. They live in the fresh air, looking for the silver lining in every difficulty they encounter. Basement people, on the other hand, are negative and cynical. They will find just about anything to complain about in their dreary, dank surroundings.

We have to be careful of basement people as they may try to suck us into their world without windows. They are egocentric and will likely try to get us to see their pessimistic view of the world and people around us. The egocentric self does everything it can to lead us farther into anxiety. Our "true self," what Williamson calls the "spiritual soul," on the other hand, does "everything to lead us into inner peace" (1992, 41). To paraphrase her, the spiritual soul is the divine's response to fear. It is the divine's answer to the ego. The spiritual soul is eco-centric.

In other words, the spiritual soul wants us to courageously love ourselves, our neighbors, our universe, from our balconies. Doing so feeds and nourishes our souls, allowing for greater internal peace and a sense of fulfillment in life.

REFLECT
Answer the following in your journal:
- Would you consider yourself a basement person or balcony person? Write down three recent examples to support your choice.
- Write down the name of a basement person you know and a balcony person you know. Next to their names, list their characteristics. What do you notice?
- What one balcony behavior can you commit to this week? Describe your experience and how it made you feel.

※※※

THE PING OF CONNECTION

Have you noticed that when you hear the "ping" of your cell phone, there is often a feeling of anticipation? *Who is texting me?* Unless we're in a conflictual text exchange or prefer to keep to ourselves, more often than not hearing that ping and seeing the name of the person texting us gives us a sense of connection, releasing those feel-good neurochemicals of serotonin and dopamine. Again, we are social beings meant to be in connection with one another. Harvard psychiatrist Robert Waldinger, in his

TEDx talk "What Makes a Good Life," agrees: "People who are more socially connected to family, to friends, to community, are happier, they're physically healthier, and they live longer than people who are less well connected" (2015).

One text reaching out to a friend or family member may make their day, giving them that sense of connectedness and belonging. All from one simple ping. *Who can you ping right now?*

✹✹✹

HAPPINESS IS A CHOICE

Being an organizational psychologist, I have worked with many executives throughout my career. Most executives work tirelessly to achieve financial success. Often that success is measured by stock prices, shareholder value—any number of financial metrics associated with their business. For some executives, this translates into eighty-plus-hour workweeks, including nights and weekends, and all too often may come at the cost of marriages, families, and health. The pressure to succeed financially can result in unhealthy behaviors, such as addictions, infidelity, poor nutrition, and sleepless nights. Some of these executives have the anxious type A personality. They tend to be competitive, ambitious, impatient, and fanatically busy, and may find themselves with little joy and inner peace in their lives. Some may not have a strong sense of self and may be triggered by other people's behaviors. In other words, they operate from fear, living egocentrically—not eco-centrically, from a position of love.

Travis Bradberry, author of the best seller *Emotional Intelligence 2.0*, cites a study by a palliative care nurse in his blog post "5 Choices You'll Regret Forever." In the study, the nurse asked patients who were three to twelve months from dying what their biggest regrets were. She found the following:

1. They wish they hadn't made decisions based on what other people thought.
2. They wish they hadn't worked so hard.
3. They wish they had expressed their feelings.
4. They wish they had stayed in touch with their friends.
5. They wish they had let themselves be happy.

Bradberry shares this in his blog:

> When your life is about to end, all the difficulties you've faced suddenly become trivial compared to the good times. This is because you realize that, more often than not, suffering is a choice. Unfortunately, most people realize this far too late. Although we all inevitably experience pain, how we react to our pain is completely under our control, as is our ability to experience joy. Learning to laugh, smile, and be happy (especially when stressed) is a challenge at times, but it's one that's worth every ounce of effort. (2015)

I often share these revelations of the dying with my clients, particularly those unhappy executives living in fear. If they chose to push through their fears and focus on love, on loving themselves, loving others, and on being loved, perhaps they would feel more peaceful and fulfilled with the love and connection they have in their lives.

In *The Book of Joy,* the Dalai Lama and Archbishop Tutu concur with living a simple life:

> When we see how little we really need—love and connection—then all the getting and grasping that we thought was so essential to our well-being takes its rightful place and no longer becomes the focus or the obsession

in our lives. We must try to be conscious about how we live and not get swept away by the modern trance, the relentless march, the anxious accelerator. (2016, 97)

We have a choice to either move forward with love and create joy and peace in our lives or stay stuck in unhealthy patterns and behaviors of the past. What will you choose?

※※※

HAPPINESS THROUGH LOWER EXPECTATIONS

As human beings, we tend to put expectations on one another, especially the important people in our lives. We put expectations on our spouses, best friends, parents, sisters, and brothers. We think that because they hold special roles in our lives, they *should* behave in certain ways. Don't they know the important person protocol? I have been disappointed too many times when my important persons didn't show up as I expected them to. *What do you mean you can't attend our wedding? How are you not by my side when I am going through chemo?*

Yet, these expectations aren't really fair. Where did they come from? More often than not, they are societal expectations. Based on what we hear from friends, family, movies, and social media, our important persons are *supposed* to behave in certain ways. And when they don't, we feel many emotions—hurt, frustrated, angry, sad, disappointed, etc. But please know that most often their behavior doesn't have to do with how they feel about us. Try not to take it personally. Whatever the disappointment, it typically has to do with what's going on in their lives, or how far along they are in their journey toward enlightenment. We will experience greater happiness if we keep our expectations in check. Happiness through lower expectations works every time.

I recently had a conversation with my dear friend Lynn. We were commiserating over the fact that each Mother's Day and Father's Day we feel quite disappointed with our children's behaviors and attitudes, having to remind them several times *an hour* that "it's a special day." The long and short of it, we concluded, is that these "special" days are not all that enjoyable. Our expectations are inevitably too high.

"Chris and I have decided that we are no longer going to celebrate Mother's and Father's Day. We're done. We feel like it will be more peaceful for all of us," Lynn shared laughingly.

Brilliant, I thought. Happiness through lower expectations, especially with our kids.

❋❋❋

PERFECT IS THE ENEMY OF GOOD

As I have shared, fear is a natural human condition that we all experience. But if we allow it to stifle us, we remain exactly where we are today, stagnant from lack of growth. If, instead, we push through it, we are learning and growing along the way, even if we sometimes fail. We learn more from our failures than from our successes, yet fear of failure is all too common for most people. And why wouldn't it be? Throughout our years of schooling, we are taught to seek perfect scores—A-pluses, if you will—not failures or Fs. Fast-forward to our professional careers, and we have the same heavily ingrained mentality: seek *perfection* and avoid *failure* at all costs. This is hard to "unlearn," but we must try; striving for perfection is stressful and *elusive*.

We could stand to learn some lessons from entrepreneurs who know that the fastest way to success is to "fail fast and often." Failure is *not* a weakness, but rather suggests that we were bold enough to try something new, different, out of our comfort zone, and push through that fear and our discomfort. It takes courage to be imperfectly perfect.

REFLECT

Below is an exercise you can try to "unlearn" perfection and fear of failure and rewire your brain for courage.

- Take up something new–e.g., mountain biking, singing, yoga, golfing, baking, painting; it really doesn't matter what it is. Notice that you won't be perfect at it the first time or even the twentieth time. It will take a lot of practice, and over time you will see improvement and growth. Your brain will begin to register that proficiency is not a first-try occurrence. It takes making mistakes, learning from them, and more and more practice.
- Be gentle with yourself, knowing you are courageous to forge ahead with a growth mindset, leaving perfection and worries about failure in your rearview mirror.

❄❄❄

ON THE ROAD TO ENLIGHTENMENT: FIRST STOP: COMPASSION

Before I had cancer, I would find myself annoyed by some people. I had a short fuse too often, sometimes with challenging customer service reps, slow drivers (I am from Boston, after all), and those who were disrespectful to others. I could also fall into the victim mode too quickly as was clearly evident in how I reacted to my cancer diagnosis, and Dr. Reece in particular.

After my fight with cancer, and finding faith, I still have to learn to *choose* love over fear *daily*. When I choose love, I am much more patient with myself and others, rarely speaking out in anger or frustration. I am more in control of my emotions and thus less affected by them. Helping those around me, and my greater community, gives me a sense of purpose, centeredness, and fulfillment. I feel a sense of lightness and enlightenment that, prior to cancer, I didn't have.

The Dalai Lama shares,

> Every day, think as you wake up: Today I am fortunate
> to have woken up. I am alive. I have a precious human
> life. I am not going to waste it. I am going to use all my
> energies to develop myself, to expand my heart out to
> others, to achieve enlightenment for the benefit of all
> beings. I am going to have kind thoughts towards others,
> I am not going to get angry, or think badly about others. I
> am going to benefit others as much as I can. (2016)

When you have the opportunity, *choose* where and with
whom you want to spend your time and energy. Often, whom
we surround ourselves with is a *choice*. We are all children of God
regardless of how we define God. There are no "bad" people, but
rather "bad" behavior. Often bad behavior stems from trauma
and suffering—something we may not be able to see or know
from someone's history.

When we encounter basement people, try to think of them
as being off their path toward enlightenment; their lives may be
full of angst, anguish, and insecurity, even if they don't realize
it. Remember, love and compassion are innate, until fear and
protection overcome them. Rather than staying angry with
people who hurt us or who have hatred in their hearts, try to
dig deep for grace and compassion for them. Know that their
unkind behavior is not about us. People who are unkind or rude
are not acting in eco-centric ways but are instead egocentric,
operating from a position of fear, not love. They feel the need to
protect themselves from some perceived threat. Treating them
with kindness can potentially get them back on track. Perhaps
they don't have a lot of compassion in their lives, and you may be
the person who gives them that opening to be their best selves,
even if just for a moment.

Of course, anger is a natural human emotion. Anger isn't "bad," but we don't want the burden of holding negative emotions in our hearts for too long. It adversely impacts us, not the other person. Once we release the anger, we are able to move forward to create the life we are meant to live. Try to remember this when at work with the grouchy coworker or behind the salty person in the grocery line. It's not about you—they are unfortunately not living their best eco-centric lives at that place and time. Try to find compassion in your heart, knowing that we are all on our own journeys toward enlightenment. Some are simply not as far along as others.

I have found this to serve me well. In *The Book of Joy*, the Dalai Lama shares his view on compassion:

> A compassionate concern for others' well-being is the source of happiness. By simply shifting my focus to another person, which is what compassion does, my own pain was much less intense. This is how compassion works even at the physical level. (2016, 47)

Research conducted by the HeartMath Institute validates the importance of letting anger go, through prayer, meditation, exercise, and/or counseling, and replacing it with compassion. The institute describes the human heart as *more* than an organ that sustains life; it also emits electromagnetic fields that change according to our emotions. This energy extends beyond our bodies by several feet and affects our connection with others.

Their research finds that intense anger increases our risk of heart attack fivefold and stroke threefold. Negative emotions contribute to our nervous system becoming erratic, wreaking havoc on the health of our bodies, while positive emotions, like love and compassion, bolster our immune system and help our brains to be more creative, innovative, and make better decisions.

According to this research, it takes *less than two minutes* to get our hearts back in balance by *simply focusing on what we appreciate and are grateful for.* Take a moment right now to focus on what you're grateful for, take several deep breaths, and notice how your body changes. I practice this several times a day and it brings me back to center whenever I feel askew.

REFLECT
Answer the following in your journal:
- Describe a time when you held on to anger for too long. How did that anger impact you or affect your life?
- Is there someone who is currently making you angry? Envision what it would feel like to relinquish that anger. Take deep breaths and start to imagine yourself in the other person's shoes. What would it feel like to choose love and compassion instead of anger?
- Martin Luther King Jr. once said, "Forgiveness is not an occasional act; it is a constant attitude." Who can you forgive today? And tomorrow? And the day after that?

✽✽✽

WHY NOT BE WEIRD WHEN NORMAL ISN'T WORKING?

Loving ourselves and each other is what matters most, not money, power, or prestige. Recently, during a sermon at our local church, our minister claimed that people who act "Jesus-like" by giving generously to others, treating all people with kindness and respect, and being patient and forgiving are "weird"—in a good way. He went on to say that "normal" people, or mainstream society, typically strive for material possessions, monetary wealth, and power. Those who are "weird" strive for something else.

Our pastor got this idea from Craig Groeschel, author of *Weird: Because Normal Isn't Working*. Groeschel argues that we humans need to be more thoughtful about how we behave in the world. Even those who claim to be believers in Christ may have lost the essence of what this really means and are caught up in keeping up with the Joneses, rather than behaving as disciples of Jesus. To turn away from such "normal" drivers of monetary wealth and power is to be "weird." Groeschel believes that given all the political strife, famine, sickness, financial disasters, and crime in this world today, being "normal" simply isn't working, so why not try something different and be weird instead?

Archbishop Tutu agrees, saying in *The Book of Joy*,

> The ultimate source of happiness is within us. Not money, not power, not status. Some of my friends are billionaires, but they are very unhappy people. Power and money fail to bring inner peace. Outward attainment will not bring real inner joyfulness. We must look inside. (2016, 14)

Williamson concurs in *A Return to Love*:

> Meaning doesn't lie in things. When we attach value to things that aren't love—the money, the car, the house, the prestige—we are loving things that can't love us back. Love isn't material. It's energy. (1991, xxii–xxiii)

And because I love my country music, why not add Zac Brown alongside the spiritual greats of the Dalai Lama, Tutu, and Williamson?

> It's funny how it's the little things in life
> That mean the most
> Not where you live, what you drive

Or the price tag on your clothes
There's no dollar sign on a peace of mind
This I've come to know
So if you agree, have a drink with me
Raise your glasses for a toast
(Zac Brown Band, "Chicken Fried")

❁❁❁

WHEN IN CRISIS, CHOOSE LOVE

A former client of mine recently went through a very difficult time. She's the executive who appears to have it all, materially—cars, homes, impressive salary, power. That said, she and several colleagues were released from their executive positions at a prominent oil and gas company after nearly twenty years with the company. The executive team and senior leadership team was restructured, which eliminated her position and others. Her supposition is that she was released to bring in younger, less expensive talent, and she's likely right; yet this is very difficult to prove, given others of both genders and various ages were released as well. When she first came to me with the news, she was considering suing the company.

My counsel to her was to go ahead and "feel all these feelings" but *ultimately choose love and forgiveness* over continuous anger and fear. Sure, she has every right to be angry and fearful of what the future may hold, but if she goes down that path, anger, resentment, and bitterness may reside in her heart and soul—perhaps permanently. Even if she wins her lawsuit, her decision to sue could result in years of negative energy surrounding her and her family. Rather than moving forward, she'll be stuck in the anguish of the past.

She has millions of dollars in her estate, so she could retire today without any financial concerns for her or her family.

Why not, I suggested, *choose* love and have a successful second act, feeding her soul with some of her passions—like her love of the ocean, kids, and sailing. Perhaps she could combine these interests into a nonprofit to serve underprivileged youth, providing sailing instruction and experiences on the ocean, I suggested. How wonderful might that be for the kids who don't typically have such opportunity and how potentially meaningful and rewarding for her? *Why not fear less, love more?*

It remains to be seen what path my client will choose, and I will support her either way, but she will certainly move through the pain much more quickly if she relinquishes her fear and anger and chooses to operate from a position of love instead.

People find themselves in similar situations all the time. There is no way to avoid pain. There is no way to avoid fear. Tragedy strikes when it strikes. We cannot control what happens to us, but we do have control over how we *respond* to the challenges we are faced with. We can *choose love* over fear and move onward and upward with our lives.

❄❄❄

"Given the scale of life in the cosmos, one human life is no more than a tiny blip. Each one of us is just a visitor to this planet, a guest, who will only stay for a limited time. What greater folly could there be than to spend this time alone, unhappy or in conflict with our companions? Far better, surely, to use our short time here in living a meaningful life, enriched by our sense of connection with others and being of service to them."
The Fourteenth Dalai Lama

❉❉❉

HEARTBEAT?

When I was nineteen weeks pregnant with our first child in 2002, Mark and I took a vacation to Cancun. I was overjoyed to be pregnant. Yet, at the same time, my sister Debbie had just been diagnosed with a recurrence of breast cancer, and a deep sadness had captured my soul. It was a true cognitive dissonance—joy and sadness simultaneously. Getting away to the beach in a country where we knew no one was something I was looking forward to.

Our first day in Cancun, I floated in the gentle waves with Mark, dreaming of the months to come. The ocean crashed magnificently on the white sandy shores. I could almost taste the salt in air. The seashore was lined with umbrellas and thatched roofs to provide some temporary relief from the sun. All I could think of as I floated on my back was how peaceful I was in that moment.

That afternoon, Mark and I were dining poolside when I started to feel ill. Within minutes of taking a bite of my quesadilla, I grew achy, crampy, and feverish. I couldn't even wait for Mark to pay our tab; I needed to lie down and went back to the room on my own.

Fortunately, the hotel had an on-site physician on staff. Thirty minutes after my symptoms began, we called him. Something, I *knew*, didn't feel right.

The doctor did everything he could to assuage our fears. "It's just the heat," said Dr. Martinez. "It happens all the time. People aren't used to the change in climate."

Dr. Martinez went on to tell various stories about how powerful the heat could be in Mexico as he examined me. "Even powerful enough to cause back spasms," he explained as he looked at my swollen lower back. He was kind and caring, but my anxiety didn't wane. I intuitively *knew* something was wrong.

When he couldn't find a fetal heartbeat with just his stethoscope, I wanted to cry. But he was confident this was normal, that the baby was fine. All I needed was some rest.

Two hours later, I hadn't slept a wink. When I saw blood in the toilet after a trip to the bathroom, I called Dr. Martinez with concern. He tried to assure me the baby was fine but that he would personally escort us to the nearest hospital in Cancun.

The second we entered the hospital, I wished I'd taken Spanish in school instead of French. I couldn't understand anything anyone was saying other than Mark: "It's going to be okay, Kat. It's going to be okay," he tried to convince me.

We were ushered into a room with an ultrasound machine, and a doctor entered, introducing herself in English as Dr. Rebeca. *Please, please, please, let me hear a heartbeat,* I chanted to myself as she probed my belly. *Please, please, please, let me hear a heartbeat.* Within minutes our baby was on the screen, her heart beating fast and steady. Mark and I breathed a heavy sigh of relief.

"See," Dr. Rebeca said, looking up at me with a smile, "the baby's fine. There's the baby's heartbeat. The bleeding is coming from your placenta. There's a small rupture, but it'll heal on its own with a few days of bed rest."

Dr. Rebeca gave me medication to stop my mild contractions and told me not to leave my bed for any reason. She was certain the baby would be okay. She left us with her pager number and encouraged us to use it whenever we needed her. She understood this was my first pregnancy, I didn't speak Spanish, and the nurses didn't speak English, and she knew I was scared. And I was. It was frightening to take pills when I didn't know what they were or what they were for, and the nurses, in Dr. Rebeca's absence, couldn't explain either to me.

Mark and I stayed that night at the hospital and woke the next morning to find that the spotting I had been experiencing had turned into a heavier discharge.

"That's normal," said the nurse. At least that's what I thought she said, but the discharge had a pink tinge to it.

This can't be "normal," I thought. Pink is *never* good; it almost always means there is bleeding happening somewhere in the body.

Mark paged Dr. Rebeca, and an hour later she walked back into my room with the Doppler in her hand. She searched for the heartbeat but this time couldn't find it. *Please, please, please, let me hear a heartbeat,* I chanted again in my head. *Please, please, please, let me hear a heartbeat.*

"Babies like to hide," she assured me, so we turned to the ultrasound, and there the baby was, just like the day before, with its tiny hands, that face, those legs. Again, Mark and I sighed with relief, but the doctor looked concerned.

"What?" I asked.

Mark squeezed my hand.

"Heartbeat?" I said urgently. "Does anyone see or hear a heartbeat?"

"No," Dr. Rebeca said. "There is no heartbeat."

The placenta, it turned out, had ruptured even more overnight when my water must have broken. The baby wasn't able to get the nutrients she needed and passed away sometime early in the morning. Dr. Rebeca believed my placenta had ruptured as a result of an infection caused by the amniocentesis I had had fourteen days earlier in Denver.

One in 500: that was the risk associated with miscarriage when I signed the amnio release form after receiving a positive triple screen result for spina bifida. Dr. Rebeca called my baby's death "a fluke." She was *so* sorry. There was nothing that could have been done to save the baby, even if she'd known my water had broken. The next step was for me to be induced and deliver the baby.

What? I thought. *Deliver the baby? Deliver the baby?*

The sadness I felt at that moment was indescribable.

❋

SPIRITUAL LOVE AFTER TRAGEDY

That day in Cancun was and still is one of the saddest days of my life. I don't even know the date. I never wanted that calendar reminder. All I know is that it was April; let's leave it at that.

After losing our baby in the midst of Debbie's battle with cancer, I was depressed. I didn't have my faith yet, so I didn't think about the possibility that things would work out as they should. Had I believed then, as I do now, that the moment my daughter's heart stopped, her spirit was one with the divine, I would have been much better off. I would have had faith that someday I would have my sons and that I would heal from the pain of losing her—*Chloe Ledet Haber*—and that one day my spirit would be with hers again. I *choose* to believe this today, having a deep spiritual love for her, which gives me a sense of peace, not sadness, whenever I think of her.

❋

HARRY

Two years after losing Chloe, we had our first son, Harrison Calvin Haber. The day he was born, February 8, 2004, was one of the most joyous days of my life. My father used to say that the love that flows down from parent to child is unique and that it doesn't flow up from child to parent in quite the same way. I think he was trying to say a couple of things when sharing this with me, but once I became a mother, I knew what he meant about the unique love from parent to child. The love that I felt for Harry when he was born was deeper and more special than anything I had ever experienced before.

Harry at three years old, and three months.

And seven months after his birth, September 1, 2004, was another one of the saddest days of my life. Debbie passed away at her home in Newcastle, New Hampshire, at the young age of forty-nine. Harry and I flew in from Denver and moved in to her neighborhood for those final months, shuffling around, spending nights in various friends' homes. Debbie found being around Harry and hearing his baby noises to be quite therapeutic. He would lie in bed with her and giggle and smile. It was hard to believe that just seven months earlier, she had been in the delivery room with me—Harry's godmother, my sister, my best friend.

Debbie and me on my wedding day.

REFLECT

Answer the following in your journal:

- Have you ever lost someone close to you? If so, describe your feelings surrounding the loss.
- Do you believe when someone dies their soul lives on? If so, what does it feel like to believe this? Close your eyes, take a couple of deep breaths, and imagine your loved one's soul being in a joyous, peaceful, spiritual realm filled with abundant love. Describe your feelings in your journal.

✳✳✳

JAKE & LUKE

Denver, Colorado, 2007

Mark and I fidgeted in the waiting room at Colorado Reproductive Endocrinology. I was pregnant. We had wanted this for some time—two and a half years, to be exact. We had a strong desire for Harry to grow up with a sibling and expand our family. Given my BRCA1 status, I knew my ovaries and breasts needed to be removed sooner versus later to protect myself against those cancers, so we wanted to accelerate the conceiving process, if possible. This round of the fertility drug Clomid did the trick. So why was I sweating?

Maybe it was because I had been pregnant five times and only one had resulted in a live birth. I had a hematoma, a sac between the uterus and placenta that accumulates blood, in all of my pregnancies. With Harry I bled for weeks. I was in my fertility doctor, Sam's, office almost every other day asking to hear that reassuring heartbeat. I could tell he was anxious too . . . until he heard the heartbeat. So much blood. How could it be possible that the pregnancy was progressing? But it was. We had a beautiful, healthy, full-term son.

With my second pregnancy after Harry, we weren't so fortunate. I started bleeding at ten weeks—another hematoma. Again, vast amounts of blood and many visits to Sam's office. He always told me to be hopeful, but I knew from his face that he had some doubt. I never liked the "we'll just have to wait and see" response. We lost the baby at eleven weeks. The other two pregnancies were similar, yet the losses were at eight weeks. There was so much heartache with each of the losses.

I have never liked those questions on medical history forms that say, "*How many times have you been pregnant? How many resulted in live births?*" It is depressing when you have miscarried.

Maybe I was sweating because after being pregnant so many times, I knew the "normal" blood count numbers to confirm pregnancy, and mine were *three* times higher.

"Hi, Sam. Success!" I said, referring to my positive pregnancy blood test results as we entered the examining room.

I had come to truly appreciate this man over our five years together. He was always caring and understanding and had dedicated many hours to my physical and emotional needs through all my pregnancies and miscarriages.

"Congratulations!" he said as he shook Mark's hand. "OK, let's get down to business." He scanned my chart and said, "We should only see one sac. You only had one follicle when you came in for your ultrasound two weeks ago."

"That's right."

I remembered the conversation Mark and I had had with him when we first came to his practice. "We really want to have another baby, but our concern about using the fertility drug Clomid is having multiples," I had said, and we all laughed. After being briefed on the low risk, we decided to move ahead.

"Hmmm." Sam looked perplexed as he scanned the ultrasound screen. "I see two sacs."

"What? Does that mean two babies?" I asked stupidly.

"Yes."

Mark followed my stupid question with one of his own. "Are you sure you aren't looking at the screen of the woman who was just here before us?"

Sam laughed. "I'm sure. Congratulations, you are having twins! Either we missed the other follicle two weeks ago, or the egg split, so we don't know if they are fraternal or identical, unless you go through an amnio . . . " he said, his voice trailing off as I shuddered at the word *amnio*.

He sent us on our way with the usual prenatal care package that I had received too many times before. He was gentle and kind, yet tentative too.

"Can you believe it? Twins?" I said to Mark as we got into our two-seater Audi TT Roadster. *This car will be the first thing to go*, I thought.

"Let's just take one step at a time," said Mark in a calm, measured tone. I wasn't sure how to take this remark.

"What do you mean by that?" I reacted too quickly, my hormones already kicking in.

"I mean, let's not get too excited about this. Let's get past twelve weeks," he said with conviction, clearly knowing the drill.

"You're right." I recoiled.

Twelve weeks later, I entered our bathroom with the familiar dread I have felt too many times before. There was blood . . . and lots of it.

"*Really?*" I cried aloud.

Twelve weeks into the pregnancy, we had moved to a high-risk pregnancy practice with ob-gyn Dr. Lindt. As Mark and I entered the ultrasound room I thought, *Oh, how I wish Sam were here*. I hated leaving his practice. Of course, it was a good thing to make it so far along in my pregnancy, but I missed Sam's care and attention.

"Two heartbeats, good. All is well. However, you have another hematoma next to the placenta of Baby A. We'll just have to wait and see," said Dr. Lindt. *Ugh, that "wait and see" again.*

"I'm sorry you are having this complication," Dr. Lindt began. "I was planning on calling you today anyway. I have the results of your early screening blood test you took last week. You have a one in thirteen chance that one or both of your babies have a severe genetic disorder. We are uncertain as to whether you are carrying identical or fraternal twins. Obviously, if they are identical, the risk is one in thirteen that both will have the genetic disorder. I recommend getting a chorionic villus sampling (CVS)—a test for congenital abnormalities—or waiting four weeks for an amniocentesis. Both will give you conclusive results. The amnio is less risky, but you have to wait four weeks."

I shook. I couldn't speak. I cried.

"I'm so sorry. I dreaded telling you this. Of all the couples we see, we were all so happy to hear you were having twins—we knew you could handle the enormity of it; I am so sorry that this is happening."

I know he thought his words were comforting, but as I heard them, I began to sob harder. Wait four weeks for an amnio? It seemed like an eternity, and more importantly, I swore that I would never, ever have an amnio again after losing Chloe. Less risk? My stomach flipped, and I ached for Chloe.

I reflected back on the last six years. I lost Chloe, my dad, and my sister; I am BRCA1 positive, and now my twins might not make it or they might have a severe genetic disorder. It was beyond overwhelming, and unfortunately I did not have my deep faith yet, so I didn't trust that all would work out as it should.

Mark and I met with the CVS specialist, Dr. Strett, the following morning. My brother George and I spent most of the night before scouring the internet, learning too much about the risks of the CVS and amniocentesis tests. Given that George lived in Massachusetts, we traded emails and drafted questions back and forth all night long. In true Mark fashion, he tried to allay my anxiety with positivity. He wanted to wait to hear what Dr. Strett had to say before letting his emotions get the better of him.

With question list in hand, Mark and I entered Dr. Strett's office.

After the exchange of pleasantries, Dr. Strett examined me.

"I wouldn't recommend the CVS. It's too risky. You are already bleeding. Your risk of miscarriage will increase substantially. There really isn't a choice but to wait another four weeks and have an amniocentesis," he said matter-of-factly.

There was that word again. *Amniocentesis.*

Holding Mark's hand, I recounted the Mexico story and my fear of having the amnio again to Dr. Strett.

"You don't *need* to have an amnio, but you need to be prepared that one or both of your babies may have the genetic disorder," Dr. Strett replied with a warmth and empathy that we greatly appreciated.

Mark and I left his office with heavy hearts. If I had had my faith at this point in my life, I would have relinquished control and my fear. I would have prayed to the divine for strength and peace, knowing that whatever happened was meant to be. But I was not so enlightened. We decided to wait four weeks and have the amnio, as difficult as the decision was, and awaited the results with bated breath. Finally, the phone rang.

"The results are negative!" the nurse exclaimed.

Tears of joy spilled from my eyes.

Jake and Luke were born on March 12, 2007, three days before my thirty-eighth birthday and six months before my lymphoma diagnosis.

Jake and Luke at three years and three months.

❁❁❁

I grew immensely through losing Chloe and through my subsequent miscarriages, as a person and as a psychologist. Now, when people go through tragedies like this, I know how to counsel them in a way that, without losing Chloe, I simply wouldn't know. I choose to be vulnerable with these clients and share my story of loss and hope, with the intent that they will feel that they are not alone and may have hope in their hearts for their own family in the future. It gives me a sense of fulfillment, knowing I am helping them. Using my challenges to support others in need brings about a deep inner peace in me.

❁❁❁

THAT DREADED LATE-NIGHT PHONE CALL

It was a cold December night in Colorado. Mark and I had moved the family back to Denver in July 2013, six years after my cancer diagnosis and after living on the ocean in St. Augustine, Florida, for three years. I'd always wanted to live on the ocean,

I'd survived cancer, Mark was retired, my mother-in-law, whom I adored, was only seventy-five miles away, and the boys were in kindergarten and preschool, so it seemed like an opportune time to make that dream a reality.

Florida had been a lovely experience for us. The Atlantic Ocean was right at our door. The warmth, the sunshine, my daily runs on the beach—it felt like a glorious extended vacation, but after three years, Mark's mom had passed, and we found ourselves missing our family and friends back in Denver. We had learned through this experience that living near our close friends and family mattered more than a beautiful geographic location.

That winter in Denver, we were living in temporary housing while our house was being built a few miles down the road in our Central Park community—a lovely, urban neighborhood with green space, communal pools, and children *everywhere*. It was exactly the community we wanted to raise our family in.

My cell phone rang at 9 p.m. I glanced at the screen and saw that it was my brother Cal. He was living in Stoneham, Massachusetts, which made it 11 p.m. his time. Cal was usually in bed by 9:30. We all knew never to call him after 8 p.m. Something, I surmised, was up.

Instead of Cal's voice, I heard George's. "Hey, Kit," George said. "Cal conferenced me in."

"OK," I said, anxiously waiting to hear what they had to say.

"I went to the emergency room today," Cal said. "I wasn't feeling great, and when I looked in the mirror, the whites of my eyes were yellow, so I went to the local hospital." He took a deep breath. "The long and short of it is that the ER doc ran a battery of tests and they found a tumor on my pancreas."

My chest tightened. Heat rose through my body, sweat already escaping from my pores. *Not pancreatic cancer*, I thought. *Anything but,* I pled. Pancreatic cancer had taken our father from us ten years prior. Now it threatened to take my brother too? It is such an aggressive cancer with a poor prognosis; the five-year survival rate is only 7 percent.

"Oh, Cal," I said, my voice cracking, "this can't be happening . . . "

"We want your opinion, Kit," George said, taking charge as the eldest, but with a slight quiver in his voice. "The doc wanted Cal to stay in the hospital overnight, but Cal wanted to go home and talk with us about what we should do next. Should he go back to the local hospital tomorrow for more tests, or go into Dana Farber, Mass General, or Beth Israel in Boston?"

I took a long breath and thought out loud. "One of the Boston hospitals for sure. It's not that much farther away, and you'll be in the best hands. I can email my doc at Beth Israel, Dr. Nichols, and see who she would recommend." As emotional as we all were, we kept that at bay, focusing on the logistics of next steps.

"That sounds good to me," Cal said. George agreed, and we promised to be in touch in the morning.

I fired off an email to Dr. Nichols right after we hung up the phone. She emailed back just hours later. She would get Cal in for a consult in the morning. I was to call her office and ask for her oncology nurse, who would have a referral to one of the best pancreatic oncologists at Beth Israel. They don't get better than Dr. Nichols.

It was very difficult being 2,000 miles away from Cal during this time in his life. He was fifty-one years old and never married. He had no children. He had four very close friends he socialized with weekly, but they could only do so much. Thankfully, George lived close by in Southborough, Massachusetts, forty minutes from Cal, and happily became his primary caretaker.

On his first visit, the Beth Israel oncologist, Dr. Jasper, after reviewing his scans, confirmed that Cal did indeed have pancreatic cancer. However, it appeared to be confined to his pancreas, which was great news. He was stage II and started chemotherapy immediately with the goal of shrinking the tumor so it could then be removed in a procedure called the Whipple, a very complex operation that removes the head of the pancreas, part of the small intestine, the gallbladder, and the bile duct, according to the Mayo Clinic.

Cal handled the chemo quite well, so we were all optimistic when he went in for the Whipple surgery in June 2014. When they opened him up, however, they saw that the tumor had grown and had already spread to the surrounding tissues. There was nothing they could do other than to perform a procedure to at least extend his life by a few months and, hopefully, allow him to digest and enjoy food until the end of his life. Apparently, 20 percent of patients who undergo this procedure have complications and cannot eat or drink afterward, and unfortunately Cal fell into that 20 percent.

The surgeon didn't share with George in advance of the surgery that he might perform this procedure, but rather used his professional judgment in the moment. George was angry when he found out that the doctor had done this without consulting him first. It would have been very easy for George to hold on to this anger and blame the surgeon for Cal's postsurgical complications. This is what we humans often do in a crisis; we become angry and fearful and choose to blame others or the world for our plight. George could have chosen this path, but he didn't. He pushed through his anger and ultimately let go of it, which allowed him to act in an eco-centric way. He took care of Cal in his final days with love in his heart rather than anger and fear.

✳✳✳

ANGUISH & SILVER LININGS

When Cal woke up from surgery and got the news that the cancer had spread, and he was therefore ineligible for the Whipple, he opted to continue chemo with the hopes of slowing the tumor's advancement. But, unfortunately, the cancer was aggressive.

Five months later, Cal passed away. It was an excruciating eleven months. He endured too much. Chemo, radiation, surgery, feeding and gastro tubes, fevers, loss of appetite, countless ambulance rides, ER visits, infections. And through it all, he never complained. As terrible as he felt at times, he was always polite to his caregivers, never forgetting to thank them for the care and support they were giving him.

I could be angry about what happened to Cal; I could be haunted by these memories. But I *choose* faith and love instead. I choose to focus on the good memories, how much we loved each other, and the special brother-sister relationship we had while he was living. Rather than focus on his last year of life, I choose to focus on the first fifty-one. And I choose to have faith that his spirit and soul live on with the divine and within me.

I also choose to focus on the outpouring of love our family experienced—the silver linings, if you will, of such a devastating loss. I was surrounded by love from so many different parts of my life: Mark; my children; my family; my Central Park community; friends from childhood, high school, college, and graduate school; Cal's best friends and coworkers; and even my high school sweetheart. No longer was I concerned with my egocentric self being "pitied." Instead my soul absorbed every single drop that was showered on me. I soaked it all in, every day that passed, every month that passed. And I gave that love right back to all of those giving human beings with an openness and authenticity that I have never experienced before.

Again, living in connection with one another is an extremely powerful biological driver. Cortisol, norepinephrine, and adrenaline are the most commonly known stress hormones, but it is not as widely known that oxytocin is also elevated in our bodies when under stress. When emitted, it motivates us to seek support. Our biological stress response *wants* us to seek support from others rather than keeping our feelings inside. Kelly McGonigal discovered this in her research:

> Your stress response wants to make sure you notice when someone else in your life is struggling so that you can support each other. When life is difficult, your stress response wants you to be surrounded by people who care about you. When you reach out to others under stress, either to seek support or to help someone else, you release more of this [oxytocin] hormone, your stress response becomes healthier, and you actually recover faster from stress. (2013)

I wish I had known this when diagnosed with lymphoma. If I knew then what I know now, I would have allowed myself to be open and accepting of the love and support that was there for me instead of being in my egocentric zone, trying to protect myself from the perceived threat of being pitied. I would have chosen to live eco-centrically, atop the beautiful balcony.

❊❊❊

SAINT GEORGE

My brother George was another silver lining in the devastating loss of Cal. I have so much gratitude in my heart for having a brother like George, or Saint George, as we referred to him throughout Cal's illness. He was selfless for those eleven months of Cal's illness. George and Cal had a very close sibling relationship; they were best friends *and* brothers. Given they both lived in the Boston area, they saw each other frequently before Cal's cancer diagnosis. They were always there for one another, in good times and in bad.

Shortly after the Whipple surgery that *didn't* happen, Cal moved in with George and his family. George continued working his demanding full-time job while also being Cal's full-time care provider. George went to *every single* doctor's appointment, even when I was in town to help out. I could've taken Cal to his treatments and doctors' appointments to give George some much-deserved relief, but that wasn't what George wanted; he wanted to be Cal's *person*. And he *was* until Cal's final breath. George was the epitome of living eco-centrically during a very difficult time.

Archbishop Tutu expresses in *The Book of Joy*,

> At some point, you will be in anguish. It does help you not to be too self-centered. It helps you to some extent to look away from yourself. And it can help make that anguish bearable. (2016, 46)

This was certainly the case for George.

George and Cal visiting me in Denver in 2005.

REFLECT

Answer the following in your journal:

- Have you known or do you know someone who has succumbed to anger and fear in the face of losing a loved one? Describe what feelings and behaviors you experienced or witnessed.
- Have you known or do you know someone who has chosen love in the face of losing a loved one? Describe what feelings and behaviors you experienced or witnessed.

✳✳✳

MY SISTER (not "half sister") JULIA

Reconnecting with my sister Julia was another special silver lining in Cal's passing. Although technically my half sister, as my mother emphasized throughout my formative years, I prefer to think of her as my *sister*. Life is too short for "half" of anything. She and I had a silly falling out around the time of my cancer diagnosis. It's too silly to recount—siblings misunderstanding each other and arguing. We hadn't had a relationship for several years; the first time I saw her again was at Cal's memorial service. We hugged and cried. No words needed to be said. We had found each other again.

She's thirty-seven years old now and married to a wonderful man. I remember when we were not in touch, I wondered if I would be invited to her wedding. The mere thought that I questioned this saddened me, knowing that my father would be quite upset with the both of us. To then be attending her wedding at the beautiful Dorset Inn in Dorset, Vermont, made my heart sing. As she walked down the aisle with her mother, Kate (my stepmother), I held back my tears of joy. As she neared the alter, she saw me, stopped, came over to where I was standing in the aisle of chairs, and gave me a kiss. My father would be very proud of us. The love was abundant. We are quite close now, a true silver lining and *choice* we both made after the devastating loss of our brother.

George and Julia on her wedding day, October 25, 2015.

REFLECT
In your journal, write down the silver linings that you have experienced in the midst of or after life challenges or tragedies you have experienced.

❋❋❋

LETTING ROMANTIC LOVE IN

Let romantic love in. This may be easy for most of us at first, but after heartbreaks and divorces and other experiences with love that ultimately don't end well, allowing ourselves to fall in love again is a difficult choice, but it is a *choice*. I encourage us to try to relinquish our fears and open ourselves up to the possibility of romantic love. I know the right person may be very difficult to find; however, there is nothing like the feelings we experience when we are falling in love, so try to be patient. Whether we are seventeen or seventy, romantic love can be quite powerful.

One of my former clients, in his early sixties, shared with me his recent experience of falling in love with one of his former outside legal counsels. When describing his love, there was a gleam in his eye and a smile on his face that he couldn't conceal—one I certainly had not seen before in the "all-business" boardroom. With a noticeable newfound energy about him, he described their countless dinners and drinks in the magical city of Manhattan and numerous long runs together in Central Park. It was a story he could hardly contain, nor did he want to.

"She just does something to me. I can't explain it. Every time we have to say goodbye, I'm counting down until we say hello. Although my days are tightly scheduled, I usually find a way to make time so I can hear her voice even if it's just for a few minutes during the day. We have a playlist that we share and listen to incessantly. I think I check my phone forty times a day to see if she's reached out to me. In case you didn't know, I'm crazy about her," he said, beaming.

I couldn't be happier for him. It takes great courage to overcome our fears. Previous to this newfound love, my former client was in an unhappy marriage, trying hard to stay together for the sake of their kids. When he and his wife decided to divorce, it was incredibly difficult, yet they both ultimately chose the possibility of a healthy love, relinquishing the fear of an unknown future.

And today he is a successful entrepreneur, building an organization with a meaningful purpose to help others in need, *and* has a personal life that is deeply fulfilling, *and* an inner peace that is palpable.

Simply put, romantic love can be incredibly special. It opens us to a different kind of intimacy than the other forms of love in our lives. The serotonin, dopamine, and oxytocin rush we get when we see or hear from our lover has no substitute. Even if we've been hurt before, let's try not to let the fear of being hurt deprive us of one of the most powerful emotions on earth.

I have many single friends, male and female, ranging from their early thirties to late sixties. Several of them speak to how happy they are being single and say they do not need a partner to make them happy. I believe this to be true. They are happy and many are quite fulfilled. Yet, sometimes we don't know what we don't know; perhaps we could feel even more fulfilled with a romantic love in our lives.

Regardless of our age, falling in love is magical. Again, we are meant to be physically and emotionally connected to one another; it's part of the essence of life, a powerful and primary biological instinct not to be denied.

REFLECT

Answer the following in your journal:

- Think back on a time when you opened yourself up to romantic love. How did it make you feel? How did others experience you?

- When have you operated from fear or gone into "protect mode" or egocentric mode in a relationship? What were your behaviors? How did it make you feel? How did your partner experience you?

- If you are single, can you commit to one action this week that will open you up to the possibility of romantic love? What will it be?

✻✻✻

COURAGE TO LET THE WRONG ONE GO

A month before I met Mark in 1998, I felt like giving up on men. I had just graduated with my doctorate in clinical psychology and had been in a relationship with a man named Doug, a handsome, sandy-blond-haired entrepreneur from California, for a little over a year. He was smart, creative, innovative, edgy, and driven to be financially successful. All the things I thought I wanted in a partner, in my more egocentric, materialistic, and image-conscious years.

Doug had arranged an elaborate graduation party for me at my boss, Kevin's, exquisite loft in downtown Denver. Kevin was out of the country and graciously offered up his home to me for the celebration. My father, mother, Debbie, and Cal had flown in for the event.

Approximately fifty people—friends, classmates, family— mingled with champagne flutes in hand on the open floor plan of Kevin's magnificent loft adorned with ancient Asian relics, Oriental rugs on wood floors, and exposed brick walls.

"Excuse me, everyone, I'd like to make a toast," Doug said, as he clinked his champagne flute with a spoon until he had the party's full attention. My father's eyes rolled ever so slightly— subtle, but enough that I noticed.

A few weeks prior, Doug had brought up to me the idea of getting married. I had some reservations. Doug had gotten married several years before to a woman to help her gain her citizenship. Being a traditional woman, this struck me as sort of unusual, but my father was beside himself when I told him about the marriage. "Immoral," he called it, to get married to anyone for any reason other than love.

Doug was also into appearances. Material things were

important to him—not a trait my father found endearing, and one that was becoming more and more unsettling to me. My father thought Doug was rather shallow, and he believed I deserved better. And down deep, I believed this too; I just wasn't quite ready to have that hard, emotional conversation with him. But I *knew* in my soul I'd ultimately have the courage to let him go. I had been proposed to once before and also *knew* it wasn't quite right given my young age of twenty-four at the time, and the need and desire to find myself. I was grateful to be able to trust that same feeling of *knowingness* years later with Doug.

Clink, clink, clink went the glass, and Doug began.

"I'll be short and sweet," Doug said. "Thanks for being here tonight to celebrate my special girlfriend's major accomplishment: earning her doctorate in clinical psychology. She's worked incredibly hard, and I am extremely proud of her. Not only is she smart and beautiful, but she's mine, hopefully for a *very, very* long time. Cheers to Dr. Kathryn Bowker. I love you."

Doug beamed with his bright Californian smile as the guests applauded.

My dad cleared his throat, standing in the back of the room, all eyes on him now.

"You took the words from me, Doug. She *is* an amazing woman, and I am proud to call her my daughter. But, Doug, I wouldn't be so bold as to think you two are a *fait accompli*," he added in his monotone voice and walked away from the crowd onto the terrace for some fresh air.

There were some gasps as the guests tried to determine whether my father was serious or not, but within minutes the cacophony continued with the infectious buzz of the evening. People who knew me knew my father was a no-nonsense sort of guy, with a dry sense of humor. However, Doug could *not* let it go.

"I am *so* embarrassed. Was your dad being serious?" Doug asked me, his light-blue eyes wide with anger.

"Yes, I am afraid he was. That's him—never afraid to speak his mind at inappropriate times with a tad of dry humor mixed in to keep everyone guessing."

"I'm going to confront him. He can't make me look like an ass in front of all these people."

"Doug, don't," I pled. "He'll come around. Confronting him now is *not* going to help." But Doug was already making his way to the terrace, where my father and brother were enjoying a martini alongside the terrace railing.

"Mr. Bowker," Doug blurted out, inches from his face, "what was that all about? Did you really mean what you said in there?"

"Yes, Doug, I did," my father replied matter-of-factly, taking a few steps back from my angry boyfriend. "One thing you didn't mention about my daughter is that she is discriminating and wise in her decisions on most things, particularly men. She's what I call a *special*; I wouldn't claim her as yours quite yet."

Doug lurched toward my father as if to strike him. Fortunately, Cal was able to get between them before it came to blows. "Back off, man," Cal said.

"Yes, Doug," I said from behind them, "please leave."

Doug spun around, aghast. He opened his mouth to say something, and I dissolved into tears.

Thankfully, he left, and I broke up with him the next day. Given how enraged he got, it confirmed to me that Doug cared most about his image, not my father, and certainly not me.

Sometimes, choosing love means having the courage to let someone go in order to find that special love.

❄❄❄

THAT SPECIAL LOVE

November 1998

After the Doug breakup, all I truly wanted to do with my

evenings was sit on my couch and watch Woody Allen movies. I had given up on men, at least for a while, and bought a VCR. One particular evening, however, I decided to meet my girlfriend and coworker Robin for an early dinner at the Washington Park Grille in Denver's Old South Gaylord neighborhood.

The brick sidewalks nestled right off of Washington Park are lined with rows of storefronts and restaurants. The Grille sits on the corner with patios flanking its north and west sides. The Rocky Mountains peak in the distance. The lights are always dim, casting an appealing orange glow on its patrons. The Grille's booths are a rich, dark wood. The fireplace roars no matter the season, and the food—Italian—is delicious and reasonably priced, especially for the neighborhood.

On that particular Monday, business was slower than usual at the Grille when we took our seats at the bar. Within minutes I noticed a tall, salt-and-pepper-haired man standing at the corner.

"Handsome guy at the far end of the bar," I whispered to Robin.

"Yup," she said. "Definitely your type."

We laughed. I *always* went for older guys.

"Mark's buying a round of drinks for the bar," said the cute but far-too-young-for-me bartender. "What'll you have?"

"Veuve Clicquot," Robin replied without hesitation.

"Don't you think you're taking advantage of the situation?" I asked, elbowing Robin in the side.

"It's a free drink. And I want champagne. I'm not drinking *swill* just cuz it's free!"

We laughed, and I ordered a Kim Crawford sauvignon blanc.

"Excuse me, Mike," I said to the handsome older man at the end of the bar. He didn't respond, his back slightly turned to Robin and me. "Excuse me," I said louder. "Mike!"

"His name is Mark, not Mike," the cute bartender said, laughing.

I blushed, but this time Mark turned our way when I addressed him by his proper name, and he approached us.

Within ten minutes, we learned he was divorced with two children. He also happened to be the owner of the restaurant. He'd just proudly celebrated his daughter's thirteenth birthday party at the adjacent Soda Shop and was glad it was a slow night "for once." He was calm, measured, and had an easy way about him.

I guessed he was ten years my senior.

"No way," I said to Robin when he excused himself to say hello to some guests at a table. If I knew one thing, I knew I did *not* want to be involved with an older, divorced man with kids.

"Oh, please. Have fun—"

Robin froze midsentence. I turned to see Mark returning with his jacket slung over his shoulder.

"I'm leaving for the night," he said to me, "but I was hoping to get your number. I don't think I have seen you here before."

Surprised but flattered, I gave him my business card. He nodded to a few employees and softly gave some instructions to the hostess as he headed out the door.

Tall. Lean. Impeccably dressed.

Too bad I wasn't interested . . .

❀❀❀

When Mark called my office and left a voicemail the next day, I plopped down in Robin's office and told her I didn't plan on going out with him. She argued he was exactly what I needed in my life—someone *not* to be serious about.

"Go out, have fun" she said. "*Have sex.*"

I loved Robin—always saying what she was thinking. I prided myself on being very discerning when it came to choosing lovers, but I thought, *She's right. A little fun never hurt anybody.*

✳✳✳

Mark picked me up that Friday night and took me to Aubergine, a lovely French restaurant downtown, for dinner and then to see a one-man play, *The Male Intellect: An Oxymoron?*, at one of Denver's small theater venues. The title always makes me smile.

While I had acquiesced to going out with Mark to "have fun," I quickly found myself intrigued by him. There was something about his peaceful sense of self that was different from others. Next thing I knew, as we sipped champagne during intermission, I asked if he wanted to have any more children—a family in my future was very important to me. When he said he did, I started to imagine what it would be like to be with this debonair, confident man who seemed to be so comfortable in his skin and had a very generous spirit.

Mark appreciated life; he was manly, and also warmhearted and romantic. He was kind and generous to everyone he came in contact with. When I asked him what had happened with his first marriage, he explained that they had an unplanned pregnancy and decided to get married at city hall a year after their daughter Rachel was born. They were both trying to "do the right thing" for their daughter. Four years later they had another daughter, Tess, yet ultimately they didn't feel compatible for the long term. After seven years of marriage they decided to divorce. There was no infidelity or any other drama—he explained that they just weren't in love. I appreciated his honesty and transparency. Before long, I started thinking he might be someone I could spend my life with.

As our dates multiplied, he proved to be as easygoing as he had first appeared at the Grille. He was fourteen years my senior, had experience and confidence, was sophisticatedly handsome, and had little ego. Though I didn't have a term for it then, he lived eco-centrically. He lived life through love rather than fear. He was a balcony person rather than a basement one. He had a beautiful heart and soul.

I was twenty-nine and Mark forty-three when I introduced him to my father over dinner at the Colonial Inn in Concord, Massachusetts, six months after we met. You might think that the age difference between us would be a problem for my father. But given he and his second wife, Kate, were fifteen years apart, he had *nothing*. My father wasted no time.

"So, Mark," he said before our server had taken our drink order, "what are your intentions with my daughter?" *Really, Dad?* I thought.

"My intention is to marry your daughter, Cal," Mark replied without hesitation, looking my father directly in the eyes.

I was stunned. It had only been six months. To be honest, I'd been thinking about it, but it hadn't occurred to me that Mark had.

"Good to hear it," my father said with a smile. "Let's order a couple martinis on that."

❄❄❄

Mark proposed to me three months later while we were vacationing on Martha's Vineyard. We married eighteen months after that in a small chapel on Cape Cod with a reception under a large, white canopy tent on the sands of Onset Beach. His daughters, Rachel and Tess, then fourteen and ten respectively, were our flower girls. The white church was filled with intimate friends and family. As my childhood minister officiated, sunshine cascaded through the stained-glass windows.

At the reception, Debbie had 3 x 3-inch squares of light-green fabric for all of our guests to write a "marriage message" on with a black felt-tip pen. After our wedding, she sewed the squares together, creating a beautiful wall-hanging tapestry for us. My father's message was in the center, and it read, "*Make* it a great life," with lines underscoring "Make." He shared with me later that life was going to be challenging at times, but I have a *choice* in how I respond, and he hoped that I would *choose* to make the best out of every difficult situation. I believe his wise advice has served me well . . . and foreshadowed this book.

Mark and I have been happily married now for twenty years. I'm grateful every day that I *chose* to let romantic love in again after having the courage to let the wrong one go.

REFLECT

Answer the following in your journal:

- Do you have a favorite falling-in-love story? If so, capture it in your journal.
- What was different about this love than other loves?

My dad and me walking down the aisle.

Mark and me on our wedding day, May 28, 2000.

LEAN IN TO LOVE

We must *lean in to love* to keep our love alive, especially when married or partnered for many years.

Friends of ours who have been married for thirteen years recently announced they are getting divorced. They have three young children between the ages of seven and eleven. We would have never predicted this news in a million years. This couple always seemed happy and respectful of one another. We spent a lot of time together over the years. They laughed a lot, and seemed to enjoy the special life they created together. With some couples, you might say, "Yep, I get it. They really don't seem to like each other, never mind *love* each other." And, divorce seems to make the most sense. This wasn't the case with this couple. When I asked what happened, they shared that they felt more like roommates than lovers. No one cheated; they just fell "out of love."

The fact is, after thirteen-plus years of marriage, and even before, we have to work at making our love last. Danielle Mitnick, Richard Heyman, and Amy Smith of the Family Translational Research Group at New York University, in a longitudinal meta-study, researched married couples and their levels of satisfaction and fulfillment in their marriage over the life of the marriage. They found that fulfillment peaks the day the couple is married and goes into the doldrums the day the first child is born and stays there until the last leaves the home. That's a long time. If we're not diligent in keeping our love alive, we may end up like more than half of the population—divorced.

The authors go on to say that during this "doldrums" period, couples often think they have fallen out of love when really this is not necessarily the case; it's just that they are so busy with the kids and the busyness of life that they lose focus on each other. Therefore, instead of assuming we're not in love, we must be deliberate and *choose* to invest in the relationship and lean in to love. This means having regular date nights, finding common hobbies, planning trips together without the kids, taking the time to communicate with each other, spicing up the sex life, and appreciating why we fell in love in the first place. Those who have been married or partnered a long time know that there may not be the same intense sexual desire with their partners as there was when they first met. The love changes over time, which can be a very good thing. The depth, complexity, and *knowingness* of each other is incredibly powerful.

Do we want to trade deep, knowing love for serial infatuation sex? This may be the reason why couples jump ship on one another. If we choose serial monogamy, we may never reach that deep, intimate, *knowing* love. If we divorce and find another long-term relationship, eventually (if we are fortunate) we will hit that thirteen-to-fifteen-year mark. The intense desirous sex may wane again. What will we do then—leave and start all over again? What about growing old with someone?

Our pastor gave a sermon one Sunday, reminding the congregation of the fact that the grass is not always greener. Instead of looking for that other garden, tend the one you have. Fortunately, according to Mitnick, Heyman, and Smith, the good news is that fulfillment in marriage takes on a whole new meaning when we are empty nesters and can spend uninterrupted time together again. We just have to make it that far. It takes energy, effort, and passion—and it's worth it. Psychologist Dr. Keith Witt's article in *Elephant Journal*, "How to Deal with the Inevitable 'Relationship Entropy,'" corroborates the findings in Mitnick, Heyman, and Smith's study:

> After the hormonal rush of romantic infatuation has passed, we become habituated to our spouse, and are vulnerable to taking our marriage for granted. If we don't consciously counteract these forces, our love, interest, attraction, passion, and commitment can slowly dissipate over the years until our marriage feels empty. (2016)

What's interesting about Witt's research is that he notes that we are "genetically programmed to habituate to our partner." In other words, from an evolutionary perspective, "we have drives to have sex, bond, raise children, but also to habituate to that person and want someone else" (Witt 2016). Instinctual drives are difficult to counteract. All the more reason to lean in both emotionally and physically. It takes hard work and dedication, but it can be done. Have date breakfasts, lunches, or dinners together, try a new experience with each other—for example, exercising, a sport, a cooking class, gardening. Share what has happened in your day with your partner and ask questions about their day. Spend a few minutes each morning holding each other before starting the day, make each other's coffee or tea, and deliver the occasional breakfast in bed. Say "thank you" more often. Touch each other—hold hands, make love. Renowned couples researcher John Gottman reminds us that we build trust and connection with our partner when we attune to their needs, sometimes at the expense of our own needs and desires. In other words, it's important to act eco-centrically with our partners, too.

Witt states, "When both partners make such efforts, long-term commitment not only works, it feels great" (2016). And Esther Perel, prominent couples' therapist and *New York Times* best-selling author, reminds us in *Mating in Captivity* that "the grand illusion of committed love is that we think our partners are ours. In truth, their separateness is unassailable, and their mystery is forever ungraspable" (2006). *Choose* to lean in to the mystery of your partner for lasting love.

REFLECT
Write the following in your journal:
- If you have been in a relationship for a long time, write down one thing you can do this week to lean in to your partner.
- Next week, describe in your journal the impact leaning in had on your relationship.
- Can you and your partner commit to leaning in on a regular basis? What specific things can you commit to each week?

Mark and me on our eighteen-year anniversary.

4

Choice #3: Choose PRAYER

PUSH: PRAY UNTIL SOMETHING HAPPENS

IF YOU ARE FEARFUL of something, PUSH: Pray Until
Something Happens. Miracles happen when we pray. I'm not
talking about feeding five thousand with five loaves of bread and
two fish or making the blind see or curing the terminally ill. A
miracle can be something as simple as a shift in perspective—
seeing a challenge or problem in a different way, through a
different lens. And, in turn, it lightens your heart. A shift in
perspective may be a calming of the mind, a shift from *"this is
terrible"* to *"breathe—let's reflect on this situation in a different
way."* When we PUSH, we allow the divine to say to us in one
form or another, *"I'm with you. We've got this together, even
through the very hard times."*

As humans, we can get mired in egocentric thinking. We
become myopic and often find ourselves in the victim role. Our
negative self-talk becomes rampant—e.g., I'll never get that
promotion; this person I'd like to ask out couldn't possibly say
yes to me; I'm not good enough; I'm not attractive enough; I'm

not smart enough—and we end up giving up before we've even faced whatever challenge or obstacle is in front of us.

When we pray, we let whatever higher power we believe in be the problem-solver, as opposed to ourselves. We essentially hand over the keys to a greater force and shut off the negative, egocentric thinking for a more eco-centric attitude. When we operate from a position of love, reminding ourselves to see the good in ourselves and others, we often are able to see or *feel* or *know* the solution. That is when answers are actually available to us—when we are open to possibility. When we're no longer fighting, fleeing, or freezing, our hearts and brains function optimally. We relax and think more clearly and can begin to tackle life's challenges one step at a time. With prayer, we re-center ourselves and are able to see our situations in a new light.

To receive this shift in perspective *is* miraculous. As Williamson shares in *A Return to Love,* it is a miracle when we *finally* can see, in a new way, a hard challenge that has been stifling us and then are able to resolve it. In other words, prayer helps us to get on that balcony and see things from a whole different perspective, out of that dank basement where we're listening to our egos and all that destructive self-talk.

✻✻✻✻

CHOOSE YOUR DIVINE

When we pray, we must pray to something or someone— anything beyond ourselves. Who, of course, is a big question for most of us. The Universe. Buddha. Allah. Love. The Divine. Shiva. The Source. Your community. Even devout Christians often wonder who they ought to pray to. God? Jesus? The Holy Spirit?

Personally, I pray to both God and Jesus (Lord). My dear friend Lydia prays to the Universe. My son-in-law, Chris, meditates to the divine each morning. In AA, alcoholics are taught to pray to the "God of their understanding," not necessarily a Christian god.

The moment we start worrying too much about whom to pray to, our prayer falls apart.

American best-selling writer and progressive activist Anne Lamott, author of *Help, Thanks, Wow,* urges us "not to get bogged down on whom or what we pray to. Let's just say prayer is communication from our hearts to the great mystery, or Goodness" (2012). Prayer helps us become more centered and one with the universe; prayer helps us become more eco-centric and less egocentric. Lamott says, "Prayer is the act of trying to communicate with the Real, with Truth, with the Light. It is us reaching out to be heard, hoping to be found by a light, searching for warmth in a time of darkness and cold" (2012). When we pray, we are looking for a way out of the dark basement of egocentric behaviors and up onto that beautiful balcony of eco-centric behaviors.

REFLECT

Write the following in your journal:

- Reflect on what is currently on your heart and mind. It could be any challenge, large or small. Describe your challenge and write your thoughts and feelings about it.
- Pray on the situation for three to five minutes. If other thoughts come into your mind, try to gently release them. Breathe deeply. Try praying for a shift in perspective, understanding, or strength.
- Try doing this a couple of times a week and then increase to once a day. Feel what happens. Record your feelings in your journal. Have you had a shift in perspective?

✳✳✳

LEARNING TO PRAY

After that first experience with prayer on the bathroom floor, I started praying every day. Just like working on my physical body with early-morning workouts, I started to work out my spiritual soul with prayer. Prayer is like a muscle; it must be pushed in order to strengthen. For me, once I got in the practice of prayer, I prayed more and more every day and slowly but surely began to find an inner peace that had eluded me most of my life. The more I worked out that muscle, the more I PUSHed myself, the better I got at it, and the more centered I became.

At first, I would kneel down by my bed first thing in the morning like my mother taught me when I was a child and fold my hands and recite the Lord's Prayer. I like the ritual of starting the same way each time. The Lord's Prayer is as follows:

> Our Father who art in heaven, hallowed be thy name.
> Thy kingdom come. Thy will be done on earth, as it is in heaven.
> Give us this day our daily bread and forgive us our trespasses,
> as we forgive those who trespass against us;
> and lead us not into temptation but deliver us from evil.
> For thine is the kingdom and the power and the glory forever and ever. Amen.

This prayer has great meaning for me. Every day I think about the fact that I don't need more than "my daily bread"—enough to live on each day. I try to live life in God's image and live without temptation or egocentric behaviors—which is not always easy, of course; I'm human!

After reciting the Lord's Prayer, I move into a prayer I came up with after listening to something similar from my pastor in Denver. He opened up every sermon with his version of this prayer. The idea of being a conduit for God to help others resonated with me.

This is my daily prayer:

> Dear Lord, I pray for love, peace, happiness, and joy.
> Dear Lord, if you can use anyone, please use me.
> If you can use anyone, dear Lord, please use me.
> Touch my heart and touch my soul, and through me speak.
> If you can use anyone, dear Lord, please use me.
> Please lead me to my life's purpose; may I live life in your image and raise my children in your image. I pray for the health and safety of my children and all of your children. May I please be on this earth for a long time to help others and myself grow.
> And, please, dear Lord, I pray to have a positive impact on another's soul today.

Then I ask the Lord to take care of the people in my life who are struggling, such as my friends who find themselves in difficult marriages, coworkers battling illnesses, even politicians who I wish would think more eco-centrically.

"Please, dear Lord," I pray, "please shed your light and love on them. May they find you and begin to find joy, peace, and healing from your light and love." Anne Lamott does the same thing. "When I pray," she says, "which I do many times a day, I pray for a lot of things. I ask for health and happiness for my friends, and for their children. This is okay to do, to ask God to help them have a sense of peace, and for them to feel the love of God" (2012, 13).

✳✳✳

NO MONOLOGUES ALLOWED

Jen Weaver, author, Christian, and public speaker, asks us to do the following in her website post "How to Pray: 5 Steps for Beginners":

> Consider how you interact with a friend, both listening and speaking. If you meet up for coffee and your friend spends the whole time talking about herself, what she wants, what she's doing, her issues, her hopes, and doesn't leave a second for you to speak or share from your heart—the relationship isn't going to last long. Come to God to hear what He has to say and to share what's on your heart. Plan space in your prayer time to listen to Him.

Prayer isn't a monologue. It's also not a place for holding back our truth. The divine knows everything there is to know about us. There's no need to sugarcoat anything or to keep any secrets. If you are addicted to alcohol or drugs, pray to the divine to help you find the strength to get healthy. If you have been unfaithful to a partner, ask for forgiveness. If you have yelled at your children, pray for greater patience and forgiveness. Remember, we're not trying to impress the divine with our lives. The divine is there to forgive us for our transgressions, not judge us. If we are honest and genuine with our prayers, and if we give the divine a chance to speak to us, peace will be more readily available. Let there be space to *feel* or *know* that shift in perspective, that *miracle*. Allowing ourselves time to listen rather than filling our days so completely that we don't have the chance to possibly hear or *feel* or *know* the divine is critically important.

❋❋❋

NO-JUDGMENT ZONE

Prayer comes in many forms. For some, it comes in the form of kneeling in a church or before bed and speaking to God. For others, it can be yoga, breathing exercises, swimming, writing poetry, *anything* that is meditative.

One day, while on my morning run, I was thinking about my sister Debbie and how much she enjoyed running too. She had passed away six years ago, yet I felt her strong presence on this particular morning. There was something about this run that was different from all my others. All my senses were heightened. It was springtime, and the smell of lilac wafted through the air. The sky was a vibrant blue with a smattering of bright-white cumulus clouds. My typical pace had increased substantially yet felt effortless. I *felt* invincible. I *felt* Debbie's presence as if she were running alongside me. I started crying tears of joy, feeling close to her and the power of the universe. I prayed on that run. I prayed for strength, I prayed for love, I prayed for guidance in this life. Soon enough I found myself praying every time I ran. It is my meditative state, and I realized I could pray anywhere at any time. So long as we center ourselves, shut out the noise, and focus with intent on whatever is on our hearts and minds, we are praying.

My point: pray when it feels right to you. Try not to make it hard on yourself. Don't judge how you connect to your source or how long you manage to pray for or what thoughts come and go as you pray. No matter what form it takes, no matter what the prayer actually is, if you make prayer an active part of your life, you will begin to feel more peace in your life. The more you communicate with the divine of your choice, the more open you will be, the more centered you will become. Try to make it a priority for yourself each day to focus on what's on your heart and mind. It's a form of self-care and preservation that you deserve.

REFLECT

Here are some ideas to help you share what is on your heart and mind:

- Present your need or intention honestly and completely. This can be done a number of ways. One method is to recite memorized prayers such as the Lord's Prayer while remaining focused on your intention, whatever is most pressing on your heart and mind.
- Another method is to converse with the divine as though He/She/They is there in the room with you. Think of the divine as a best friend you are confiding in. Remember to leave quiet time to hear, feel, or know a response.
- If you have never prayed before, try it, and describe in your journal what it feels like.

❈❈❈

WHAT TO PRAY FOR?

Praying doesn't mean that our desired answers will immediately come to us. The form those answers take may be as mysterious as the power we are praying to.

Praying to win the lottery or to achieve some elusive success are forms of egocentric thinking. It's about "me" and "I." Prayer should be about thinking beyond the self, beyond the corporeal.

If we pray to win the lottery, we might, but it's unlikely. The divine doesn't put much stock in material things. Instead, if we pray to win the lottery, the divine might answer that prayer by giving us a shift of perspective that winning the lottery is not a solution to our financial challenges. The answer might come as an awareness that it's time to look for a job that pays better. Or we might suddenly start thinking about developing our financial acumen by taking a finance class or meeting with a financial planner. Either way, the answer such a prayer garners will likely be a shift in perspective that allows us to see more clearly and, in this case, realistically or practically.

If we pray for a loved one's life to be saved from a terminal illness, this may not occur either. The divine may not spare the lives of those we don't want to die. This is not the historical times of the Old Testament where some believe that God healed them from a debilitating illness or that they prayed for the life of a loved one and, miraculously, they lived.

A more realistic answer to a prayer for a terminally ill loved one would be to begin to think differently about death. We might realize that life does not end when the body dies, but rather the soul lives on. We might understand death as a succor to our loved one's physical pain. We might suddenly see and feel that death is part of life, that death is not to be feared but to be embraced.

When I pray, I don't pray for material things. Instead, I pray for a shift in perspective, for understanding, for strength. This is not to say that we can't pray for someone going through a difficult time. As I mentioned earlier, I do that too. I like Anne Lamott's spiritual antibiotics analogy. "In prayer," says Lamott, "I see the suffering bathed in light. In God, there is no darkness. I see God's light permeate them, soak into them. I pray for people who are hurting, that they be filled with air and light. Air and light heal; they somehow get into those dark, musty places, like spiritual antibiotics" (2012).

Sometimes, the divine answers our prayers in obvious ways, sometimes in mysterious ways, and sometimes it may feel that the divine doesn't answer our prayers. When my prayers aren't answered, I give it over to the divine and assume that what I was praying for was simply not meant to be . . . and perhaps I will understand why this is as time goes by.

REFLECT

Write the following in your journal:

- Describe a time when you prayed and you felt your prayers were answered.
- Describe a time when you prayed and your prayers were answered over time.
- Describe a time when you prayed, and you felt your prayers weren't answered.
- Reflect on all three and describe what you notice. Were you praying with an egocentric heart or an eco-centric one?

✳✳✳

LAW OF ATTRACTION

As a psychologist/executive coach, I often pray for my clients. When I pray for a client, I don't ask the divine to solve their problems. I ask the divine to help me help them see their way through. I ask the divine to help them heal and to help me help them heal. Healing and seeing aren't physical or material things. They are ideas; they are concepts; they are *practices*. They aren't egocentric. They are eco-centric. Achieving the eco-centric is what prayer is about—it provides an inner peace and sense of fulfillment, knowing we are helping others; it gives greater meaning and purpose to our lives. If we constantly think of the negative, what happens? Negative things happen. We don't need proof of that. We see it every day. Author and life coach Tony Robbins says, "Where focus grows, energy flows." That's why prayer is critical. It allows us to *see* the positives by intentionally *being* positive. It's the law of attraction. Remez Sasson, a motivational and spiritual-minded author, describes the law of attraction in the following way:

> The law of attraction is the attractive, magnetic power of the Universe that draws similar energies together. It

manifests through the power of creation, everywhere and in many ways. Even the law of gravity is part of the law of attraction. This law attracts thoughts, ideas, people, situations and circumstances.

You do so through creative visualization and affirmations. By visualizing a mental image of what you want to achieve or by repeating positive statements, which are called affirmations, you create and bring into your life what you visualize or repeat in your mind. In other words, you use the power of your mind, thoughts, imagination and words.

There have always been people, from ancient times till now, who knew about this law and how to use it. They knew that repeating the same thought day after day, with interest and feeling, causes it to materialize and manifest in their lives. (2016)

REFLECT

Write the following in your journal:

- Over the next week, repeat positive affirmations while in your form of prayer, letting go of any negative self-talk. Try to do this at least twice a day.
- Describe your feelings and the outcome of the positive affirmations over a week's time, and then over a month's time.

❄❄❄

FEELING STUCK? PRAY

When I first learned from my former client I mentioned earlier that she had been released from the company she had been with for nearly twenty years, I was saddened. It's important to have boundaries with clients, but no matter how hard you try, of course you can care considerably for the lives of those you are coaching. To see this happen to her was upsetting. For several days I had a hard time sleeping and simply wasn't sure how to best help her through this very difficult time. I was *stuck*.

After a couple days of concern, I went on my daily run and realized that, somehow, I'd forgotten to pray about her. How could this be? Whenever I can't square something, I give it up to the divine and ultimately come to a healing shift in the way I am thinking. But instead, my emotions had gotten the better of me, and I was in my egocentric place: *Why hadn't the CEO, whom I had coached for years, consulted me before making the organizational leadership changes? Did he not value my perspective any longer?*

I was in "me" mode, concerned about why my thoughts on the restructure weren't considered or why I was not confided in; I was not thinking eco-centrically. I finally recognized I needed a shift in my perspective, so I prayed about it.

"God," I said as I ran my six-mile Central Park loop, "please help my client see the light. Please help me help her to have faith that all will be okay in the end. Please help me help her believe she and her family will make it through and will be okay. Please help me help her make choices from the balcony and get out of the basement. And please let me let go of the hurt I am feeling from not being consulted by the CEO before the final decisions were made."

And voila, almost immediately, I had a shift in perspective. I let go of my hurt feelings, realizing that this was certainly not about me; there could be a number of legitimate reasons why I wasn't consulted that had nothing to do with me or my relationship with the CEO. I also knew the supportive words to share with my former client. I *knew* to coach her to choose faith, love, and prayer, instead of lawsuits that consume too much money and negative energy. I became confident that she would have a wildly successful second act, after experiencing all the emotions she was experiencing. And today she *is* healing, deciding to *choose love* in the end.

❋❋❋

PRAYER JUST FEELS GOOD

Prayer can help us achieve a sense of centeredness in our daily lives and a shift in perspective on a particular struggle. Prayer is also a great way to deepen our faith; it is a vehicle of faith. If we have a rich prayer life, we will become closer to our divine, and we will feel supported. It's almost like having a best friend around us all the time. There is great peace in knowing that we have this relationship we can always access and count on.

Prayer also just feels good. It helps me feel as though I serve a purpose: to do good in the world and help others overcome unexpected life challenges. When I pray, I feel I am living my life in the divine's image, aka love. When I'm not acting or behaving in the divine's image, I feel less centered or grounded; I feel stuck. I often say to myself, *This is not how I want to show up in the world.* When I start feeling this way, I recognize I need to get centered again, and I gain that center through prayer. Sometimes when I lose patience with my kids, I will close my eyes, take a deep breath, and pray to the divine for greater patience. Simply focusing on the desire to be calm and compassionate centers me, and I am able to be more gracious within moments. Prayer can be as informal as that. It leads to greater faith, which in turn leads to a greater practice of love in everyday life.

When I pray for a friend or client, it feels good to acknowledge that I'm trying to be supportive of the person through prayer—it gives me a sense of fulfillment. Even before I believed in prayer, when someone learned of my cancer and said they would pray for me, I felt a sense of love and support. I felt like part of a community, which was meaningful. I'll never know if I survived my cancer because of their prayers, but I'd like to believe that the divine heard those prayers for me.

Author and theologian C. S. Lewis chose to believe in the power of prayer in his book *The Efficacy of Prayer*:

> I have stood by the bedside of a woman whose thighbone was eaten through with cancer and who had thriving colonies of the disease in many other bones as well. It took three people to move her in bed. The doctors predicted a few months of life; the nurses (who often know better), a few weeks. A good man laid his hands on her and prayed. A year later the patient was walking (uphill, too, through rough woodland) and the man who took the last X-ray photos was saying, "These bones are as solid as rock. It's miraculous." (1958, 2)

Lewis adds, "But there is no rigorous proof [of the efficacy of prayer]. You need not, unless you choose, believe in a causal connection between the prayers and the recovery."

Although no proof of the efficacy of prayer exists, when I *choose* prayer, I feel more centered, peaceful, and fulfilled. Why argue with that?

❖❖❖

IF PRAYER ISN'T YOUR THING, MEDITATE

Whenever you feel like you have very little control, it's important to remember that you *do* have control over some things:

1. Your beliefs
2. Your attitude
3. Your thoughts
4. Your perspective
5. How honest you are

6. Who your friends are
7. What books you read
8. How often you exercise
9. The type of food you eat
10. How many risks you take
11. How kind you are to others
12. How you interpret situations
13. How kind you are to yourself
14. How often you say "I love you"
15. How often you say "thank you"
16. How you express your feelings
17. Whether or not you ask for help
18. How often you practice gratitude
19. How many times you smile today
20. The amount of effort you put forth
21. How you spend/invest your money
22. How much time you spend worrying
23. How often you think about your past
24. Whether or not you judge other people
25. Whether or not you try again after a setback
26. How much you appreciate the things you have
(Gunner, #LIFEHACKS)

In addition to this list, we have control over being able to hit our internal "reset" button and *silence our minds*. When we silence our minds, we connect to a deeper level of consciousness, what Deepak Chopra describes as "our source." This may seem too far out there, but stay with me. What harm can a bit of silencing of the mind do? In fact, think of the potential benefits to both mind and body.

When we connect to "our source"—a deeper level of consciousness, similar to a deep, dream-free sleep—our bodies come back to homeostasis or equilibrium. Our heart rate, brain activity, and stress hormones are impacted in positive, healthy ways, much like what happens when we cool down from exercise or a startling experience. The evidence of this has existed for centuries, in various cultures. In this deeper level of consciousness, or silence, we allow for greater amounts of love, compassion, grace, security, acceptance, and optimism to be present and flow. Who wouldn't want that?

So, how do we go about silencing our minds and connecting to our source, that deeper level of consciousness?

Meditation—specifically a mantra meditation. Repeating your mantra in a quiet place allows you to go deeper into meditation and access a deeper level of consciousness. The mantra replaces your other thoughts. It draws awareness away from your busy brain and its thoughts and feelings, allowing for a deeper sense of peace, opening yourself up to the love, compassion, grace, security, acceptance, and optimism that I mentioned above. Deepak reminds us that silence is the birthplace of creativity, possibilities, joy, and peace (2020).

Your personal mantra is a word or phrase that speaks to you, something that aligns with your core values. It may be as simple as "peace," "compassion," "gratitude," "breathe," or the Hindu "Om" (the primordial sound of the universe). When you repeat your mantra in your head silently, it creates a space for you to slip into a consciousness separate from the chatter of your thoughts. Start easy, just a few minutes each day, and work your way up. Thirty minutes of meditation has been proven to have similar psychological benefits to a full night's sleep. Why not give it a try? You may find it to be a powerful tool during challenging times.

5

Choice #4: Choose
DIVINE INTERVENTION

DIVINE INTERVENTION, AS DEFINED in this chapter, can be as simple as a shift in perspective brought about by prayer, the divine speaking to us through thoughts or feelings of *knowing*, or by people in our life who are meant to cross paths with us so they can share their experiences that will help us on our own life's journey.

I believe some people we meet come into our lives for a reason. Some stay longer than others and have a true impact. Some are meant to teach us a lesson. Sometimes the lesson is a hard and challenging one and sometimes it is positive and joyous. Some people come into our lives to share how they've gone through difficult times similar to what we may be currently experiencing. They are meant to guide us or to be supportive. And sometimes people enter our lives to show us what *not* to do.

Marshall Segal, author, seminary graduate, and managing editor of desiringGod.org, shares this in his article "Prayer for Beginners":

On any given day, God may choose to move or speak in some unexpected way through his spirit, bringing something to your mind, altering some circumstance, saying something through a friend. People are brought into our lives at just the right time to help us through similar experiences, challenges. This is God listening to us. (2016)

✳✳✳

SPIRIT GUIDES

Similar to Segal, past life regressionists and many spiritual leaders believe we have spirit guides who whisper notions and insights that may seem like our own and yet are influenced by a higher power. Spirit guides are exactly what they sound like: spirits who guide us in our lives. They provide us with insights and thoughts that we otherwise would not experience. I'm not suggesting we all have angels sitting on our shoulders, but I do believe we are guided by the mysterious—that voice that suddenly speaks to us, that inexplicable nudge that tells us to do something or say something.

Our thoughts are *our thoughts*, of course, but where those thoughts come from, how they are formed, can be guided by the divine, the universe, or whatever or whomever we choose to have faith in.

Sometimes, out of the blue, I'll think about someone I haven't seen or talked to in some time, and I'll reach out to them. More often than not, the person will respond back with a version of "Your intuitive sense is uncanny; I've been having a really hard few days. I'm glad you reached out." Was it my random thought to contact this person? I could think that way. But instead I *choose* to believe the divine had a hand. It gives life *meaning* and *purpose*, something every human being needs to live a fulfilled life.

❋❋❋

JUST A FULL-SIZE BED

When my mother was diagnosed with stage IV pancreatic cancer in July 2015, we were saddened and stunned by the news. Of all cancers, she was diagnosed with this one—the one that took her ex-husband and son. It is unusual that she had the same disease without being a BRCA gene carrier. However, if she could have choreographed her exit strategy from this life, she'd want to exit the same way as her ex-husband, the one and only love of her life—and did. So, in this regard, perhaps we shouldn't have been surprised by her diagnosis. Indeed, there are those who believe that we do choreograph our lives before we are born. Who knows?

My mother died five months after her diagnosis, thirteen months after losing her son, my brother Cal. Given her age of eighty-two and how advanced the disease was, she opted for only limited radiation treatment. She had tumors in her abdomen that manifested as open sores over most of her stomach. Other than the discomfort of having a nurse change her bandaging twice a day, she was actually in very little pain, which was a true blessing.

During one of my last visits with her, my mother and I were at the Mount Vernon House, a beautiful Victorian, seventeen-room assisted-living facility in Winchester, watching the Patriots football game and eating takeout burgers from the local Blackhorse Tavern. She was feeling pretty well, considering. She started to get tired at about 7 p.m., so I told her I would tuck her into bed and say good night and head over to Diane's (*"I want to be your person"* Diane) to spend the night. She agreed, and after I hugged her good night and walked out the door, I *felt* this strong inexplicable desire not to leave, as if my spirit guide was guiding me to turn back.

I went back inside and lay down beside her until she fell asleep—something I had *never* done before in my adult life or throughout her illness. She fell asleep peacefully, with my arms wrapped around her. I cried softly, knowing how much I would miss her when she was gone. As I lay there with her, I remembered many, many nights when I was a child and had a bad dream and found my way to her room and slept with her all night long—always with my foot touching hers, so I knew she was close. I thought she had the most enormous bed ever. But as we lay together I thought it was funny that her bed was just a full-size bed. It was simply because I was so small when I was a child that I thought her bed was enormous. *Thank you, Mom, for always being there for me—and for all of us,* I thought. She passed away a week later.

My mother recounted this story of me lying in bed with her to a few of her close friends, who relayed it to me at her memorial service. She told them it meant a great deal to her that I came back and stayed with her until she fell asleep. *Thank you, spirit guide. It meant so much to both of us.*

My mother and me on her seventieth birthday at the
Waldorf Astoria in NYC. Debbie was taking the picture;
the three of us were in Manhattan for a long weekend
seeing a Broadway show and taking a carriage ride around
Central Park—something my mother had always wanted
to do. Don't let me fool you: my mother was a frugal
person. This was a special treat her children planned in
honor of her seventieth.

❋❋❋

SOUL GROUPS

A soul group is what it sounds like: groups of people with souls that attract each other. If you've ever met someone for the first time and had an immediate comfort with them, as if you've known them your entire life, you know what I'm talking about. This has happened to me several times in my life. In fact, two friends have said almost the exact same thing to me shortly after we met: *I know we just met, and I don't know all of your facts and figures, but I feel I know your soul.* I felt the same way.

I had to laugh the other day when a girlfriend of mine said she has an acupuncturist whom she feels she has known all her life. "I feel like I'm at *home* whenever I'm in his presence," she said. "Is that strange?"

I was able to reassure her that it wasn't strange at all.

"The same thing has happened to me," I told her. "*Several* times. Perhaps he's in your soul group."

My friend raised her eyebrow. "Really, Kathryn? *Soul group?*"

I laughed. "I know," I said. "It sounds a little New Agey as a psychologist, but I believe in this." And we know from the law of attraction and quantum physics that our energy frequency and vibrations attract "like" energy frequency and vibration.

Spiritual author Remez Sasson describes how the law of attraction works beyond the practices of visualization and affirmation I mentioned earlier:

> The law of attraction manifests through your thoughts, by drawing to you thoughts and ideas of a similar kind, people who think like you, and also corresponding situations and circumstances. It is the law and power that brings together people of similar interests, who unite into

various groups, such as political groups, sports teams, sports fans, fraternities, etc. (2016)

Why not soul groups too? I went on to tell her about several friends I have who I believe are in my soul group and gave her a few examples.

My dear friend Susie is most certainly in my soul group. We met in the third grade and *got* each other right away. Susie moved from Pittsburgh, Pennsylvania, to Winchester, Massachusetts, where we grew up down the street from each other from the age of ten. When we met, I immediately felt a closeness to her, like she was a sister. We both felt an instant comfort with each other. Not only did we think similarly, we were both extraverted and enjoyed socializing with many different types of people, even the adults in our lives when in our teens. We had a deep empathy for people, and as adults our chosen professions turned out to be quite similar. She's a social worker; I'm a psychologist. Our insights about life seemed to be profound to one another whenever we discussed them. This sort of relationship doesn't happen every day. No doubt she's a member of my soul group.

Susie and me in Denver in 2018.

She sees life through kitty colored glasses

**Susie gave me this plaque a few years ago, playing off
my nickname Kitty (and Kit) from my childhood and my
thoughts on choosing to *make* it a great life.**

The same thing was true ten years later, when I met my college roommate, Lydia. The first time we met I felt like I had known her my whole life. Conversing was easy with her. Thirty years later, we still talk several times a week, and we talk about anything and everything. Many of our conversations are about relationships and spirituality. She has great insights that always seem to apply to my life. It's as if time stands still when we are together. I consider Lydia to be another member of my soul group.

According to mystical writer Raven Thomas, "When we're drawn to another person for seemingly no reason, it's usually a sign that an individual is a member of our soul group" (2016).

Raven goes on to describe seven signs that indicate you've met someone from your soul group. If you know someone who checks all of these boxes or most of them, they are likely a member of your soul group.

1. You feel as if you've known them your whole life. It's a level of comfort you never expected to have with someone so soon.
2. You have had similar life experiences, and they help to show you new ways of handling old problems.
3. You lose track of time around them. In fact, time seems to stand still when you are together. It's as if the whole world only consists of you two.
4. They have surprising wisdom and insight. You find yourself constantly surprised by the profound words that come out of their mouth, and how everything perfectly applies to your life.
5. They show you the best in you and reveal the beauty in yourself that you never realized was there. They teach you how to turn your weaknesses into your greatest strengths.
6. When they come into your life, it is right when you need it the most. Chances are, you won't fully understand this

until you both go through the experience you were meant to, together.

7. They help you to learn lessons you thought you had already conquered and show you the hidden meaning within. Some lessons are painful, but your soul group helps you every step of the way. (Thomas 2016)

REFLECT

Write the following in your journal:

- Reflect on these seven signs and ask yourself who in your life checks most of these boxes. It could be someone from the past you haven't seen in years. It could also be more than one person.
- Describe the relationship you have with this person. What does it feel like to be in their presence?

✻✻✻

AN AFFAIR, FOLLOWED BY AMAZING GRACE

Sometimes people come into our lives at the exact right moments, particularly if we PUSH.

Take my girlfriend Kim, another member of my soul group. We've been friends for over seven years, ever since I moved back to Denver. We like to say we are soul sisters; we felt an immediate connection the first time we met. Whenever we are together, we never run out of things to talk about. Our time together is always too short.

I have referred to Kim's family as the J. Crew family. She's beautiful (inside and out), and she married a nice-looking attorney over twenty years ago, and they have three terrific kids—smart, well mannered, gracious. And appearance-wise they always look like they walked out of the J. Crew catalog—natural beauty, well dressed in preppy, vibrant colors with bright smiles on their faces. From outward appearances the family seemed as close to "perfect" as a family could get. Until several years ago . . .

That's when, on a walk together, Kim told me her husband was having an affair. I stopped in my tracks and chills went up my spine. This was the *last* family I thought this would happen to. It's a stark reminder that we can never truly know what a family is going through by mere observation.

It was very unfortunate the way Kim found out about her husband's infidelity. Her kids saw an inappropriate iPad text message from the woman her husband was having an affair with. When Kim confronted her husband, he confirmed he'd been having an affair for months and had no plans to end it. He showed neither remorse nor regret. In addition to this emotional blow, he had recently lost his salaried, executive-level job, and was attempting to find career success as an entrepreneur while driving for Lyft. He decided to relinquish the majority of his parenting responsibility to Kim, which left her with very little support for the day-to-day needs of their three young children, and little financial stability. Needless to say, Kim was saddened for her family and for the loss of the life she thought she had.

Throughout the hurtful divorce that followed, Kim and I spent countless hours in conversation about the importance of choosing faith, love, prayer, divine intervention, and vulnerability each and every day. It's what she had to do to be her best self for her children. Of course, she was very angry when she first learned of the affair . . . who wouldn't be? But ultimately, she chose not to hold on to that anger, as she knew it would not be in her best interest or her children's.

Kim likes to say I showed up in her life right on time, but she also came into my life at just the right time. Supporting her as a friend greatly informed the way in which I counsel my clients going through similar experiences. Every married person knows that there is always the possibility of being tempted by alternatives—we're human after all. Marriage and parenthood, at times, is harder than we can ever imagine or be prepared for. But remember, we have to lean in and tend the garden. I learned from Kim's experience that being open with our partner about the struggles we have as families is crucial to a healthy relationship. Honest communication and vulnerability are critical. If Kim's husband had been open with his feelings about their relationship and marriage before having an affair, perhaps they could have avoided much of the pain and hardship for their family, even if the end result was still a decision to divorce.

As difficult as Kim's experience was, today she is able to make something of her grief and help others who are going through their own challenging divorces. She is making this life challenge count by choosing to be vulnerable and share her story with others. Her resiliency and grace are tremendous. In the years that followed, Kim allowed herself to let romantic love in, and found a wonderful partner, and chooses to live life from the balcony. She recently gave me an embroidered tapestry that reads, "Your heart and my heart are very, very old friends" and a beautiful homemade Soul Sister card for my birthday. A soul-grouper, for sure.

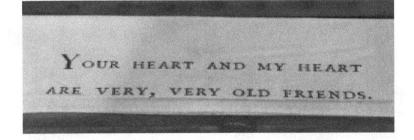

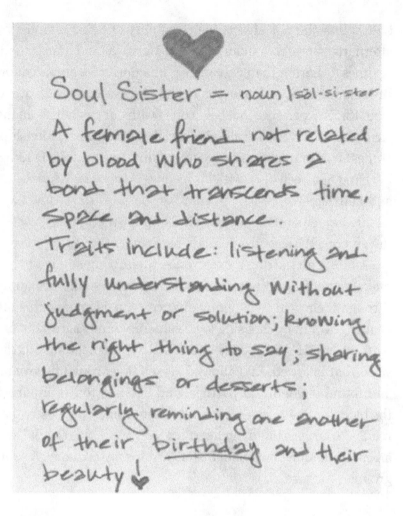

Soul Sister = noun |sōl-si-ster
A female friend not related
by blood who shares a
bond that transcends time,
space and distance.
Traits include: listening and
fully understanding without
judgment or solution; knowing
the right thing to say; sharing
belongings or desserts;
regularly reminding one another
of their birthday and their
beauty ↓

❋❋❋

NEAR-DEATH ENLIGHTENMENT

Dr. Eben Alexander is a neurosurgeon who once did not believe in life after death. Like many scientists, he didn't put any weight in the notion that consciousness exists outside of brain function. That is, until he contracted spontaneous E. coli meningitis, a disease that impacts fewer than *one* in ten million people per year and is almost always fatal or results in permanent neurological deficits.

Alexander ended up in a coma for seven days. While in his coma, he had a profound near-death experience (NDE), a spiritual encounter where when close to death you feel detached from the body and experience a variety of sensations such as levitation, security, and peace.

According to Alexander, he made a "complete and remarkable" recovery, which he shared with the world in his *New York Times* best-selling book *Proof of Heaven*.

Today, Alexander believes that true health can be achieved only when we realize that God and the soul are real and that death is not the end of personal existence but rather a transition. He writes in *Proof of Heaven*,

> Near-death experiences, and related mystical states of awareness, reveal crucial truths about the nature of existence. Simply dismissing them as hallucinations is convenient in the conventional scientific community, but only continues to lead them away from the deeper truth these experiences are revealing to us. The physicalist model embraced by many in the scientific community, including its assumption that the physical brain creates consciousness and that our human existence is birth-to-death and nothing more, is fundamentally flawed. (2012)

Alexander believes his NDE was meant to happen to him so that he could convince other physicians that there is indeed an afterlife. *Proof of Heaven* has allowed Alexander to touch millions of people who have nothing to do with the medical community. I read it years ago before Cal was diagnosed with pancreatic cancer. When Cal was dying, I *knew* it would provide him much-needed comfort to hear Alexander describe an afterlife. And it did provide comfort; we listened to the audiobook together in his final days.

Alexander is no longer a practicing neurosurgeon. He now writes books on spirituality and has speaking engagements all over the world to talk about his beliefs. It took courage and vulnerability to share his story. He put his reputation on the line by taking a public stance on a subject that will always be controversial. Today he has a successful second career and has positively affected the lives of people across the globe.

Alexander believes that it wasn't coincidence that this happened to him. God chose him, a neurosurgeon, to contract this very rare form of meningitis and fully recover from it without neurological impairment—a true miracle, and from my perspective, divine intervention.

❋❋❋

NOTICING OTHERS

When we moved back to Denver in 2013, I met Kendra. Her son and my son Harry were in the fourth grade together. Our boys instantly became close friends and spent a lot of time together. As a result, Kendra and I spent a lot of time together too and enjoyed each other's company.

When first meeting Kendra, I noticed she was very thin. She'd been a long-distance runner, so I assumed that was the reason for her body composition. Then it dawned on me one day that I never heard her talk about running. Being a runner myself, I was curious about whether we might run together sometime. When I asked her, she said she recently had developed arthritis in her right foot and hadn't run in over a year, which made me think, *Why so thin?*

I tucked that thought away for a few months until Kendra and I went to the pool one Saturday afternoon with our boys. We were both in bikinis, and I was feeling self-conscious. I kept thinking, *I'm not sure I can pull this off anymore in my mid-*

forties. And with Kendra I couldn't help but think in the other direction—she looked *too* thin.

A few weeks later, I dropped her off at her home after a school meeting we'd attended. She was sharing some frustrations from her week and I gently asked, "Do your frustrations and stresses impact your eating? I've noticed you're really thin." I had learned through my coaching sessions over the years that you can ask almost anything of anybody, as long as you do so respectfully and from a loving, compassionate place.

She looked at me with wide eyes and quickly teared. She then shared with me her decades-long struggle with an eating disorder. I listened intently and then invited her over for tea the following afternoon. After hours of discussing, I suggested she consider a treatment program for her eating disorder. Fortunately, after some thoughtful deliberation, she decided to get the help she needed. She courageously went into a partial hospitalization program followed by an intensive outpatient treatment program, totaling six months, and now, over five years later, she's doing exceptionally well. She's not fully recovered and continues to participate in support groups and therapy, but she's maintaining a healthy weight, and she is noticeably less anxious about the challenges of daily life. Kendra could have denied her eating disorder when I asked her about it, but instead she decided to be vulnerable and share her story with me. I am so glad she did, for herself, and her family and friends who love her.

Recently, Kendra and I went out for a drink and she told me she believed I was placed in her life for a reason. She said she questions whether she would be alive today if it weren't for me encouraging her to get treatment. "Meeting you wasn't a coincidence," she said. "It was divine intervention. You came into my life right when I needed you most." My heart skipped several beats and we hugged, tears in our eyes. She and I continue to be dear friends today, which I am very grateful for.

✳✳✳

THE CANCER COACH

I met Lyle over a decade ago when I was asked to be an executive coach for a leadership development program for a Fortune 1000 construction company.

When I first met Lyle, a project manager in the program, I asked him about his professional pursuits as well as how things were going for him personally. I take a holistic approach to coaching—honoring the whole person and whatever they are experiencing personally and professionally. I believe you cannot separate the two. What happens to you professionally affects you personally, and vice versa, so both are open for discussion during my coaching sessions.

It turned out Lyle had a lot going on in his personal life. His dear wife, Kaylene, had been diagnosed with breast cancer. He was worried about her health and wasn't sure how their two young daughters were coping. Given my experience with cancer, I was able to give him a perspective that others in his life couldn't give, specifically about the importance of spending as much time as possible with his wife and daughters through this difficult time.

"Work will always be waiting for you," I said. Then I shared some of my experiences with my and my family's cancers. "I spent as much time as I could with my loved ones before they passed away, and when I had my own cancer, I made sure to be with my husband and my boys as much as possible," I said. "I have no regrets . . . and I didn't lose my job. You may be surprised how understanding your company may be if you're open with them." We talked for a few hours.

And that was that. Our session ended, the leadership development program only lasted a few days, and I returned home to Colorado.

Six years later, I got an email from Lyle. This is what he

wrote: *Dear Kathryn,*

> I'm not sure you remember who I am. I've attached a couple of emails to spark your memory. I wanted to reach out and say thank you. We only spent a few hours at the Leadership Development Program. So, you will never know how much you did for me. I can't express my gratitude enough for your words of support and encouragement you gave me. During one's lifetime, I believe you meet a few extraordinary people that, if we were paying attention, greatly enriched and saved our lives. To me, you are one of these people.
>
> And I wanted you to know that. I've always meant to stay in touch and of course, life got in the way. Kaylene passed away in late August. It was a difficult couple of months and I wonder when the pain will end. My focus is on the girls. They're 12 and 15 now. Everyone keeps telling me, take care of myself, but you and I know that isn't really in my DNA. I will, though, as the girls are depending on me. I wanted to let you know that the guidance you gave me served me and my family well over the past few years. It made the time Kaylene and I shared the best it could be. I hope this email finds you and your family well. Thank you for your kindness and the positive influence you had on my work and personal life.

I couldn't help but cry when I read this email, feeling blessed and truly humbled to have touched his life. Today, Lyle and I trade texts several times a year, catching up on each other's lives. I choose to believe it was divine intervention that I was the coach assigned to Lyle for the leadership program. There were twenty other coaches he could have been assigned to, but it was me—*the cancer coach.*

REFLECT

Think of times when people have entered your life at just the right time, even if you didn't realize it until later. Think of people whose lives you have entered just when they needed you. Write the following in your journal:

- Make a list of these people. How did you help each other? What did you learn from one another?
- We could think of these "chance encounters" as exactly that, chance, but instead describe what happens and how you feel when you choose to believe these experiences were divine intervention.

❈❈❈

AN UPGRADE AND A SALAD SHORTAGE

Several years ago, I was a partner at RHR International, a global consulting firm that provides executive coaching and leadership assessment and development for executives, among other services. The work was intellectually stimulating, but after two years with the company, the seventy-plus-hour workweek and weekly travel to my clients' sites in other states was draining. Given the losses in my family and my BRCA gene, I didn't want to spend so much time away from my family; I didn't want to be like some of those executives who look back at their lives and wish they had done things differently.

There are some mothers who enjoy the travel associated with their professional careers, which I certainly respect, but I have always preferred to be at home with the boys and Mark as much as possible. I love being a mom—even the day-to-day mundane activities like going to the grocery and running errands—but my work schedule didn't allow me much time to do those things. I was missing out on school activities and the boys' sporting events, things that mattered to me very much.

There's a connection and experience that you create when your kids are young that only happens in the *now*. I knew I couldn't get that time back.

Given this, I started to think about looking for a different career opportunity when I was on the way home from a meeting in Washington, DC. I had just finished interviewing a potential candidate for a vice president position for one of my clients in the medical device industry. After the half-day interview, I planned to write the assessment report for my client on the airplane while it was still fresh in my mind and to maximize my time during air travel. That way when I got home to Mark and the boys, I could spend my time with them, not writing the report.

When I checked into my United flight, I saw that I had a middle seat in the back of the plane. Given that I'm 5'11," middle seats are already tough, and I wasn't looking forward to trying to write my assessment report on a tiny tray table in between two people, with all my notes and testing reports in hand. So, I decided to upgrade to first class, which in the last two years with RHR I had never done.

I found myself with a window seat in first class with plenty of room to stretch out and write my assessment report. Thankfully, the gentleman next to me had earbuds in and was engrossed in his reading, not appearing to be the gregarious type. It looked like it would be a productive flight.

"Excuse me," the flight attendant said as I typed away. "Would you like the paella or the salad?"

The gentleman next to me and I ordered the salad and went about our business of reading and report writing.

A few minutes later, the flight attendant returned to inform me that they had run out of salads and asked me if I wanted the paella instead. Clearly, I didn't have the same frequent-flier "status" as my fellow first-class passengers, all of whom had received their desired entrees, which made me laugh.

"No, thank you, I'm fine," I said, refusing the paella, at which point the gentleman turned to me and said, "I'll take the paella. You can have my salad." I turned to see that he had taken out his earbuds and was now focusing his attention on me.

"That's very kind of you," I said. "Are you sure?"

"Of course," he said. "What are you working on there?"

"An assessment report. I interviewed a candidate for a VP position for one of my clients, and now I'm making a recommendation as to whether I think she's a good fit with the team and company culture."

"Really," he said. "That's interesting. Who do you work for?"

"RHR International," I said. "It's a global consulting firm of business psychologists." Then, for some reason, I added, "I love what I do, but my ideal job would be to work for a mission-driven company as their internal psychologist and executive coach."

"Really," he said again. "I'm Rob Strain, president of Ball Aerospace. I wonder what it would take for you to consider coming to work for us?" he quipped.

Over the next three hours, we talked about his business and my twenty years of experience with coaching and leadership development. We talked about the assessment report and what was included in that process. My perspective is just a data point among other variables in the hiring process, I explained, but one bad hire was worth hundreds of thousands of dollars— hence why companies invest in consultants like me.

Rob explained that the aerospace industry was going through significant growth, particularly at Ball. His team was very strong, but he wanted a resource that could support them during their tremendous time of growth.

"Great meeting you," I said as we deplaned.

"You realize that was a three-hour job interview," he said with a smile as we shook hands and I gave him my business card. "I know, I know," he said. "Some people say they're going to be in touch and you never hear from them again, but I *will* be calling you next week."

And he did.

After a more traditional interview with Rob and several of his team members, I started with Ball four months after our meeting on the plane. I've been with Ball for over two and a half years now as their executive coach. My colleagues and team as a whole are well-intentioned, healthy leaders with strong, admirable values and a passion to make a difference for our nation. Our culture is people-centric, or eco-centric, which ultimately helps bring about solid business results. Our growth in the last couple of years has been unprecedented, and the work we do for our country is noble and impactful. I am very grateful to be a part of the Ball family.

I could choose to see that seat upgrade and the salad shortage as serendipity, but what would I gain from that? I choose to believe I was meant to upgrade to first class that day and sit next to Rob. I choose to believe that the divine put me in the right place at the right time and answered my prayers. I hadn't prayed for a new job per se, but I had prayed to spend more time at home with my family, to get back to writing this book, and to serve others through our church and by facilitating cancer support groups—all things that were put on hold while working for RHR, and which today I am doing.

And for the record, I also believe my girlfriend Jill didn't just "happen" to be in the neighborhood the morning of my PET scan, nor did Debbie's oncology nurse Janine just "happen" to be transferred to the hematology floor the day of my first chemotherapy appointment, nor was it happenstance that Dr. Peters's colleague was filling in for him the day she strongly recommended that I have the entire lymph node removed to know for sure whether it was cancerous or not. I believe divine intervention was at play; they were all meant to be there for me.

✳✳✳

IN THE SKY

Back in 2003, when Debbie's breast cancer had returned, I was on a flight back to Denver from Boston after a visit with her, sitting next to a Harvard Medical School cancer researcher, who fortunately didn't have earbuds in and wanted to converse. I was thirty-four years old, pre-kids. I shared with this man, Alex, that I was very worried about Debbie's prognosis, and described her cancer history and her Dana Farber treatment plan. After discussing, he asked me if I had been tested for the breast cancer genes. I had heard a little bit about the BRCA1 and 2 genes, but I didn't think they pertained to me given that no one else in my family besides Debbie had been diagnosed with breast cancer or the other associated cancers. As we chatted throughout the flight, Alex educated me on the BRCA genes and their importance in repairing damaged DNA, and how the cancers associated with the gene mutations were aggressive cancers.

I told him I didn't think I would get tested, that it all felt too overwhelming. He encouraged me to reconsider. As the plane landed and we deplaned, he was a few passengers ahead of me when he turned around and yelled above the cacophony, "Kathryn, *please* get tested." There was something about the intensity of his eyes and the assertiveness of his voice that made me reconsider.

And three months later, I did. And I tested positive for the BRCA1 gene. Again, I believe I was meant to sit next to Alex, a Harvard cancer researcher, on that flight. If I hadn't met him, I would not have gotten tested when I did. If I never learned of my BRCA1 mutation, I would not have had the prophylactic surgeries. Would I have been diagnosed with breast or ovarian cancer? Would I know to get screenings for pancreatic and colon cancer and melanoma? Alex was a blessing. He was put in my life right when I needed him most.

✻✻✻

STARFISH ABOUND

Debbie loved the beach and shared this love with me at a very young age. There are plenty of photos of me—even in the cold winter months, in my purple parka with a fur-lined hood at the age of three—walking with her on the sands of Crane Beach on the North Shore of Massachusetts. This was one of our favorite spots throughout the years. There is a castle there that sits high upon a hill, overlooking the beach and ocean. I often thought I'd marry there. It was a spectacular setting appropriate for my love of the ocean and a young girl's fantasy of beginning happily ever after.

On one of my beach excursions with Debbie at the age of fourteen, I found an exquisite starfish dried to perfection in the warm August sun on Crane Beach. I kept that starfish and it began my collection. Real, glass, gold, silver—it didn't matter what form; they all were part of my assortment. My father would shop for me every Christmas at DeScenza's Diamonds in downtown Boston. I have countless pieces of jewelry from there, but only the gold starfish pendant, unusually large in size and intricate in detail, is a favorite of mine, donned often, some thirty years after receiving it.

Debbie was the matron of honor at my wedding. I gave her two gifts to commemorate the event. The first was a sterling silver Tiffany's starfish pendant, which we both wore on my wedding day. The second was a trip to Cancun that we would take together in September, four months after my May wedding. Given our love of the ocean, I figured it would be just what we needed, some sister time on a white-sand shore and out of the cold of Colorado and New Hampshire.

The starfish has come to have more meaning to me throughout the years. As a psychologist, I appreciate the symbolism of its rejuvenation and regrowth. We humans are not perfect and can feel broken at times. However, if we *choose* to heal, we can replenish, grow, and rejuvenate our souls just as a starfish regrows its arms when wounded.

And, as a psychologist, I resonate with anthropologist Loren Eiseley's parable of the starfish in his essay "The Unexpected Universe":

> One day a man was walking along the beach when he noticed a boy picking something up and gently throwing it into the ocean. Approaching the boy, he asked, "What are you doing?" The youth replied, "Throwing starfish back into the ocean. The surf is up, and the tide is going out. If I don't throw them back, they'll die." "Son," the man said, "don't you realize there are miles and miles of beach and hundreds of starfish? You can't make a difference!"
>
> After listening politely, the boy bent down, picked up another starfish, and threw it back into the surf. Then, smiling at the man, he said, "I made a difference for that one." (1969)

Perhaps this story subconsciously influenced my daily prayer to have a positive impact on one person's soul each day. If I can make a difference for one person in a day, I've *made* it a great day.

When we moved to St. Augustine, Florida, in 2010, the boys were three, three, and six years old. My lymphoma was behind me, as were my prophylactic surgeries. Mark and I thought living on the ocean would be a great way to replenish our souls after a tough few years. All of us, except Harry, are Pisces, born in March, and have an unwavering affinity for the water. Our first month there, I gave the boys a challenge.

"I'll pay a dollar for every starfish you find on the beach today." Given I hadn't seen any starfish on the beach before, I thought this was a low-risk proposition and a fun activity to do in between playing in the ocean.

Wouldn't you know, the boys found *forty-eight* dried starfish on the beach that day! And in the three years that followed while living on Vilano Beach in St. Augustine, we never found another one. To me this was a sign from the divine that, like the starfish's imperfect arm that heals itself, I, too, would heal my heart and soul on the ocean in St. Augustine—which I did, as I was on my faith journey at that time. Divine intervention is everywhere, if you look for it.

One of the forty-eight starfish. Yes, we still have it ten years later.

※※※

LEAVE COINCIDENCES AT THE DOOR

Recently, I had lunch with a high-powered female CEO. We had been introduced by a mutual friend nine months earlier and had spoken on the phone, thinking there might be a synergy between our businesses. She reached out to me to see if we could meet for lunch.

Within a few minutes of meeting, I intuited that something might not be quite right with Celia. She seemed ever so slightly distracted, like her mind was not completely focused on our meeting.

After we ordered our lunch, we started talking about our personal lives, and within minutes her eyes welled with tears, and she told me she was going through a painful divorce with the love of her life. She was in deep despair, had lost twenty pounds over the last year, and was doing all she could to keep it together for her two teenage boys. *Ah, no wonder the slight distraction,* I thought.

I shared with Celia my thoughts on choosing faith, love, prayer, divine intervention, and being vulnerable to share our stories. She took notes as we spoke, barely touching her lunch. At the end of our hour and a half together, we hugged, and she shared that our conversation was exactly what she needed in her life at that particular moment.

Not long after, I received a beautiful bouquet of white tulips, which happen to be my favorite flower (they were the centerpieces at my wedding). When I opened my email, I found that she'd written me. "I truly enjoyed our lunch," she began.

> I find it amazing what comes at you when you need it most. I have thought about our conversation a number of times, and even brought it up during fellowship after church service this past Sunday.
>
> While kicked in the gut last week, I have truly come to realize God/the Universe has a greater plan for me. Tom is the love of my life; however, I can't do his work and I can't control what is happening. It is time to take care of myself, my boys, and move my life forward. (NOTE: Don't let this statement fool you; the grieving is horrific.)
>
> I am a big believer in love, authenticity, and vulnerability—and, like you, I wouldn't want the connection to be any other way. As scary as it can be, you have to put yourself out there . . . and once you do, you start to see what comes back to you when you need

it . . . and what you are able to help others with when they are in need.

Thank you for listening to me. It was so nice to meet you! I look forward to seeing you again soon.

I was grateful that even through her pain and sadness, she was able to be authentic and vulnerable with me—and open to leaning in to romantic love when the time is right. Since that lunch, Celia and I have developed a lovely friendship, which I am grateful for. I don't believe our meeting was coincidence.

If we choose to look for it, suddenly we see divine intervention everywhere, even in places we would least expect . . . such as at last year's Ball Aerospace Turkey Trot. Each year Ball sponsors a 5k race for its employees and their families on Thanksgiving morning. It costs fifteen dollars per person to enter, all the proceeds of which go to selected employees in our company in financial need due to medical expenses. One of the recipients of last year's Turkey Trot money shared this note with our team:

> I want to thank you so much for the proceeds from the Turkey Trot. It seems that I need a piece of medical equipment that insurance will not cover. The check I received was the *exact* amount of the device. I couldn't believe it. It warms my heart knowing people care.

The *exact* amount? That seems too implausible for me to believe it was a coincidence.

When we start looking for divine intervention, we don't just see it in our own lives; we see it in others' as well.

Recently, a colleague of mine went to get his hair cut from his regular hairstylist, who was having a trying day. She explained that she had to move out of her current housing situation and was having difficulty coming up with the required deposit on a new apartment. She was also having a hard time with her parents, who were not being emotionally supportive but instead rather hurtful toward her.

Later that evening, as my colleague discussed his hairstylist's situation with his wife over dinner, he was struck with an idea: he could prepay the stylist for a year's worth of haircuts and provide her with some much-needed financial relief. This would give her enough money for her deposit and perhaps would provide her with some emotional support as well.

The next day, he dropped off the check to her. She was overcome with emotion at his generous gesture. Fast-forward two months later, and she is in an apartment thanks to having money for the deposit, and she is thriving. His act of kindness not only helped her out of a financial crisis, but it also restored her faith in the everyday goodness of people.

When my colleague told me about this experience, I smiled knowingly. He's a very kind person, but paying it forward like that was not an everyday occurrence for him. Perhaps his spirit guides were at play.

REFLECT

Answer the following in your journal:

- What one eco-centric act of kindness can you commit to this week? These small acts of kindness can mean so much to another soul.
- Describe how it felt for you to express this act of kindness.
- When have you noticed divine intervention in your life? When have you observed divine intervention in other peoples' lives? Describe your experiences and feelings.

✳✳✳

ANGEL ALLISON

My dear friend from elementary school, Allison, was diagnosed with breast cancer a year after my lymphoma diagnosis. We were both living in Newburyport, Massachusetts, and our boys were the same age. The way she handled her diagnosis was very different from how I handled mine. As I shared earlier, when I was diagnosed, I was in egocentric victim mode, telling very few people about my diagnosis, not wanting to be pitied. Allison, on the other hand, was very open with her diagnosis, and as a result, an outpouring of love and support continuously surrounded her—a great example of living eco-centrically (her), not egocentrically (me). After two years of treatment, her cancer was in remission.

After Mark and I and the boys moved back to Denver, I made sure to visit her whenever I traveled back East.

I got a call from her in 2013, tearfully sharing with me that her cancer had returned after six years in remission. We were devastated, knowing that after a recurrence the prognosis for survival was typically three to five years.

After hanging up the phone, I cried for her and her family and for knowing all too well that recurrence could happen to me at any time.

Leave it to Allison: She chose to live each day to the fullest rather than in despair. She decided to leave her job as an insurance broker and dedicate each day to her family and friends and battling the disease. She traveled and appreciated life. She chose faith, love, prayer, the divine, and vulnerability every day. Allison was grace incarnate.

July 2018, five years after her recurrence, I arranged to visit Allison in Newburyport the day after the wedding of one of my closest friends since elementary school, Kara. Our annual family reunion on Cape Cod was moved back a week so that I could be Kara's maid of honor.

The day following the wedding, I drove to Allison's home, apprised by her CaringBridge site (a website that allows friends and families to stay connected on health-related events) that "home care was on board." Knowing Allison, this was code for hospice.

When I arrived, her living room was adorned with blue and white hydrangeas and violet roses in various vases. She lay in a hospital bed, no longer having the strength to get out of bed, with a morphine drip by her side. She was as lucid as ever, enthusiastically asking questions about Kara's wedding and my family. She spoke with conviction and love that afternoon, without any fear or regret. She showed me a notebook of letters prepared for various special occasions for her boys as well as a video she and her husband had made for them.

"Allison," I told her, holding her hands as I sat on the edge of her bed, "Debbie's sons were the same age as your boys when she passed, and they talk about her *all* the time. They remember *everything* about her. They've *never* forgotten their mother, and they have turned into fine young men. Debbie's spirit surrounds them and is in them. Your boys will *never* forget you either. Your spirit will be with them and in them, too."

Allison's face lit up. Her smile was as broad as I had ever seen. Her eyes twinkled. "Thank you, Kit, for saying that. It means so much to me."

Allison passed away four days after our visit.

I believe it was divine intervention that I was in town *that* week and was able to express to Allison that, based on my experience with Debbie and her boys, her sons would never forget her. I am overjoyed I was able to share that with her and see her magnificent smile.

I will choose divine intervention every time; it gives me a sense of purpose and peace.

Allison in 2016 attending a Wings of Hope fundraiser for pancreatic cancer research in Stoneham, Massachusetts.

Kara and me on her wedding day in July 2018. I love that there is almost twelve inches between us in height.

❊❊❊

CRAVING PURPOSE

Choosing to believe in divine intervention—that the divine has chosen to speak to us through friends, or by bringing something to mind, or through an encounter that shifts our perspective—is an important choice we can make on a daily basis. Choosing to believe in a higher power that listens to our prayers over believing in coincidence or serendipity allows us to see our world and to think about our lives in more purposeful ways. We pay more attention to what comes up in our lives and who is in our lives and *why* they are there, for better and for worse. It helps give life more meaning and purpose. The psychology is clear on this; without purpose, human beings suffer, as explained by Dr. Steve Taylor in his blog the *Power of Purpose*:

> The need for purpose is one of the defining characteristics of human beings. Human beings crave purpose, and suffer serious psychological difficulties when we don't have it. Purpose is a fundamental component of a fulfilling life.

Choosing coincidence or serendipity over divine intervention would not provide fuel for my everyday life. However, choosing to believe the universe puts some people in my life for a reason *does* fuel me. Along with having faith in the divine, love in my heart, and prayer to center me, this choice nourishes my soul.

6

Choice # 5: Choose
VULNERABILITY

SHARING OUR STORIES

WE ALL HAVE UNIQUE histories. Our lives and the stories that come from them are like our fingerprints: they are uniquely ours. When we share our challenges—large and small—with others, we make what we have gone through mean something beyond ourselves. When we share our stories, we help others feel less alone. They realize others have experienced something similar, and perhaps they then have hope that they will get through their challenge, too. When we are vulnerable—defined by Brené Brown in *Daring Greatly* (2012, 34) as being uncertain, taking risks, and being emotionally exposed—and share our stories, we are living eco-centrically rather than egocentrically. We are thinking more about others than ourselves.

Yes, it takes courage to share our story. Yes, it takes vulnerability. But vulnerability and authenticity lead to greater connections with others. Remember, we are biologically wired to be in connection with one another. This connection leads to a more peaceful, fulfilling life when we choose to be on the balcony, operating from love and compassion.

It may take years on the other side of your life challenge to be able to express your story. There's nothing wrong with that. As I shared, when I was diagnosed with lymphoma, I didn't want most to know my plight. At that point in my life, I still cared about what people thought of me, and I was very much in egocentric mode, doing everything I could to protect myself from the outside world's judgment. It took me five years to start sharing my story. No matter how long it takes, I encourage you to share yours. Sharing is therapeutic. It is cathartic. It is communal. It has been all of these things for me.

The Dalai Lama and Archbishop Tutu agree with using our challenging experiences for something good:

> As you grow in your spiritual life, whether a Buddhist or a Christian or any other tradition, you are able to accept anything that happens to you . . . . There are going to be frustrations in life . . . . How can I use this as something positive? (2016, 39)

❀❀❀

OUR CHALLENGES HAVE MEANING

In Rick Warren's book *The Purpose Driven Life*, he states, "The very experiences that you have resented or regretted most in life—the ones you've wanted to hide and forget—are the experiences God wants to use to help others" (2002, 310).

Life is hard on us all, but there are lessons in our challenges. Every difficulty we encounter has a purpose. It helps us to build our character. If you think of your life as a story worth sharing, you will see how each and every challenge is a step toward a deeper you rather than a crisis you do not deserve. As I said, it took me years to begin to be vulnerable by sharing my story, and I feel gratitude that I did if it can make a difference in the lives of others experiencing their own challenges. Growth doesn't happen overnight, but if we are open to being vulnerable and sharing our life experiences, we will see how it not only impacts others in a positive way but also contributes to our own growth.

※※※

THE WHOLEHEARTED

In Brené Brown's TED Talk "The Power of Vulnerability," she describes her years of research and hundreds of interviews, and how she learned that those who have a strong sense of love and belonging *believe* they are worthy of love and belonging. She calls these people the "wholehearted." She says that the "wholehearted" have the courage to share their stories with their whole hearts. Not half their hearts. Not some of the hearts. Not with half-truths and omitted details. "These folks have the courage to be imperfect," she says. "They fully embrace vulnerability. They believe what makes them vulnerable makes them beautiful." Brown goes on to say that the way to live with vulnerability is to give up control and instead embrace vulnerability because "vulnerability is the birthplace of joy, of creativity, of belonging, of love." I couldn't agree more.

Vulnerability is about our humanness, the willingness to be comfortable with not being perfect. It is very powerful and freeing when we can give up the notion of needing to be perfect or right all the time and accept ourselves for who we are—strengths and weaknesses alike—and are willing to share this with others. Again, it takes courage to be vulnerable. But the connections we make and the relationships we can build as a result of being authentic and open can be life altering.

REFLECT

Answer the following in your journal:

- Describe a time when you were vulnerable. What was the situation?
- How did it make you feel to be vulnerable? What was the outcome of that vulnerability?

※※※

THE COLE SUKLE AWARD

The Cole Sukle Award is given to a player on our son Harry's Little League team who exemplifies leadership and sportsmanship both on and off the field. It is named after Cole Sukle, a fourteen-year-old boy on the Eagles baseball team back in 2012 who was killed by a drunk driver. The Sukle family tells their son's story every year through the presentation of the Cole Sukle Award. Harry was the proud recipient of the award several years ago.

The Sukles express their vulnerability by sharing their story to honor their son and to teach us how drunk driving can impact lives in ways we can't imagine. From the loss of Cole, the Sukles help save lives. They do not host a big presentation where they speak to a large audience. They have not written a book about Cole. Instead they share their message through a beautiful certificate and the history of the award.

Those who are familiar with the award learn about Cole as a person and how he passed away. Most impactful stories have an important lesson to learn, and the Cole Sukle Award is no exception. It highlights the importance of leadership and teamwork from an eco-centric perspective, educates on the potential devastation of drinking and driving, and opens our hearts to Cole's parents for sharing their pain and making a difference in the lives of teenagers and their parents.

✳✳✳

AIDAN'S PLAYGROUND

A friend of mine from elementary school, Matthew, lost his ten-month-old son, Aidan, several years ago to a tragic drowning accident. As you might expect, he and his wife experienced tremendous grief after such a devastating loss. A year after Aidan's death, they had a playground built in Aidan's memory, "Aidan's Playground at Castle in the Trees," in Littleton, Massachusetts. Matthew and his wife could have chosen to dwell in the basement but instead chose to stand on the balcony where there is light and hope on the horizon and tell their son's story with a park named after him. They chose to operate from a position of love and to be vulnerable for the sake of themselves, their family, and their community.

For Matthew and his family, Aidan's Playground provides a feeling of peace when they see children laughing and playing on that playground. Of course, they will always bear a great sense of loss over Aidan, but they also experience joy—because they told their story and helped give back to their community, which in turn helped them in their healing process by putting love back into their hearts. Matthew and his wife recently welcomed a baby girl into their family—a true miracle after experiencing so much pain and grief, and a testament to the impact letting go of fear and replacing it with love can have.

✳✳✳✳

A TRAGIC ACCIDENT

A former client and friend of mine, Jay, got behind the wheel after a long day of hunting with his dad. They had had several beers throughout the day, and on their way home, Jay missed a turn and crashed his car into a stationary train while driving approximately sixty miles per hour. Tragically, his father died instantaneously, and Jay ended up in intensive care for several weeks.

Jay hit *his* rock bottom when he woke in the hospital and was told what had happened. Not only did Jay lose his father, but to make matters worse, he was also charged with vehicular homicide in his father's death. Jay was devastated. Beyond the grief he experienced after losing his father, he was fearful that he would lose his wife and family if he went to jail. In despair, he was open to the hospital chaplain's request for a visit with him.

Lying in intensive care, with the help of the chaplain, Jay started to pray. Right then and there, he prayed for forgiveness and grace . . . and he, too, felt a sense of peace overcome him, much like I had on that bathroom floor. After serving one month in prison, Jay returned to his family and began to rebuild himself. He served five months of house arrest and ten years of probation. Fortunately, the company he worked for, Lawson Software, stood by him, choosing to operate from a position of love rather than judgment. Ultimately Jay became CEO of Lawson until he resigned in 2005.

Today Jay shares his story as a highly successful keynote speaker, executive coach, and consultant (www.coughlanconsulting.com). His story gives him the opportunity to change the lives of others while simultaneously helping him heal and grow as a person. The connections he makes with his audience are powerful, and often, after he presents, audience members approach him with their stories as well. It's cathartic and fulfilling to share your story and to help others share theirs in return. It's human connection at its best, and provides our lives with that greatly needed purpose.

✳✳✳

MISCARRIAGES AND IVF

Recently, I had lunch with a former client named Faith. She is a private and reserved person, a self-described perfectionist who believed she had always been in control of herself and her destiny. She openly admits she is not comfortable showing vulnerability. After I shared with her the five choices we can make to move through our fears and not just survive life's challenges, but truly thrive, she asked if she could share something very private with me. "Of course," I said.

She went on to tell me that she has had three miscarriages in the last few years. One of her losses was twenty weeks along. All three miscarriages were devastating, she said, adding that she and her husband were considering IVF after their most recent loss several months ago.

My heart went out to her immediately, and as divine intervention would have it, I was able to share with her my loss of Chloe at nineteen weeks, and the spiritual love I ultimately chose. Faith shared with me her own experience of relinquishing control of the conceiving process and putting her trust (or faith) in a higher power. For the first time in her life, she had to accept that she did not have control over her situation. She could be vigilant about taking good care of herself, but ultimately, she could not control whether she would be blessed with a biological child.

This was all very reminiscent of my cancer experience and my loss of control. We spent two hours discussing her situation and my journey through loss and fulfillment I had experienced from learning to be vulnerable. We both left with faith and love in our hearts, thankful for the discussion we'd had.

Faith emailed me the next day.

"I am so appreciative of your openness and support," she wrote. "Our conversation gave me such hope and definitely makes me feel humbled by all the loss and challenges you have overcome. Perspective can be such a powerful tool."

The Dalai Lama and Archbishop Tutu agree with putting our situations into perspective to help mitigate our worry and anxiety, as they express in *The Book of Joy*:

> You can think about others who are in a similar situation or perhaps even in a worse situation, but who have survived, even thrived. It does help quite a lot to see yourself as part of a greater whole. (2016, 99)

Faith took the chance of being vulnerable with me, and as a result it brought her hope. Our shared vulnerability created a sense of community that allowed us to further our healing. And, from my perspective, it was another example of divine intervention.

While choosing to be vulnerable to others might materialize as a public demonstration—for example, in books, while public speaking, or building a playground—it is equally valuable if you tell your story more privately; it can be as simple as a discussion over lunch. Not all of us want to share our stories with the masses, even if we have the platform. The important part is to choose vulnerability and tell your story, no matter the form, the platform, or the audience. Others will be grateful for it, which in turn nourishes our souls and gives us a sense of purpose.

REFLECT

Answer the following in your journal:

- Do you have a life challenge you can share with another in your way? Describe that challenge and how you might tell the story.
- Describe a time when someone expressed vulnerability and shared their story with you. What was that story and how did they tell it? How did it make you feel?

❋❋❋

MY NEMESIS: PANCREATIC CANCER

Maureen Shul, founder and executive director of Wings of Hope for Pancreatic Cancer Research in Colorado, lost her mother and brother to pancreatic cancer within months of one another. In 2012, with no experience in nonprofit organizations and driven entirely by grief, she founded a nonprofit for the sole purpose of funding pancreatic cancer research. Having lost my father, mother, and brother to pancreatic cancer, I was asked to be on the board of Wings of Hope for the same reasons as Maureen—to raise awareness and funding to fight this devastating disease that took our loved ones from us. Today, Wings of Hope is in partnership with the University of Colorado Cancer Center, Anschutz Medical Campus, providing annual research grants to help find a path forward to a cure for pancreatic cancer.

At every Wings of Hope event, Maureen shares the pain and grief of losing her mother and brother. Without expressing her vulnerability and grief, her story would not be complete. That vulnerability and openness has resulted in Wings of Hope raising close to one million dollars to date for pancreatic cancer research. Not only does it give us hope for a cure in the future, but also, for those of us who have lost our loved ones to pancreatic cancer, it is meaningful to know we are not alone; we have a connection to one another, similar to the connection I experienced with other cancer patients at Dana Farber when being treated for my lymphoma.

Although the connection to others through Wings of Hope is a somber one, it's still an immediate connection and bond. Again, the human condition prevails, providing a sense of peace and fulfillment that we are there for each other and *know* each other's pain. As Glennon Doyle shares in *Untamed,*

> Heartbreak delivers your purpose. If you are brave enough to accept that delivery and seek out the people doing that particular world-changing work, you find your people. There is no bond like the bond that is forged among people who are united in the same world-healing work. (2020, 269)

Maureen has had a tremendous impact on so many by sharing her story and founding Wings of Hope.

✸✸✸

INDEPENDENCE OR INTERDEPENDENCE?

Keynote speaker Jeremy Poincenot was declared legally blind from a rare genetic disorder at the age of nineteen. He competed in and won the 2010 World Blind Golf Championship and more than ten international tournaments since then. He describes how prior to going blind he was a very self-sufficient, independent young man who did not rely on anyone. He felt his independence was a badge of honor and was quite proud of it, similar to how I felt before being diagnosed with cancer.

When he suddenly lost his eyesight as a sophomore in college, he also lost his independence. He needed to rely on others to help him with many daily tasks, and certainly to compete and succeed as a blind golfer. Through his experience, he now recognizes the power of *interdependence*. He has said, "I can honestly say I'm happier today at twenty-seven years old, legally blind, living interdependently, than when I was at nineteen years old fully sighted, trying to be as independent as possible." He encourages others to not be afraid to ask for help. His experience taught him that people enjoy and find purpose and fulfillment when they help others in need—it's a two-way street. It is not a sign of weakness; quite the contrary. It brings about connection to one another, that neurobiological need. Jeremy helps others by sharing his story and the important lessons he learned thus far in his young life.

※※※

RAW VULNERABILITY

In the book *Carry On, Warrior*, Glennon Doyle shares her twenty-year struggle with alcoholism and bulimia. On Mother's Day 2002, unmarried and addicted, she learned she was pregnant. "For the first time in my life," she writes, "I wanted something more than I wanted to be numb. I decided to become a mother and vowed to never again have another drink, cigarette, drug, unhealthy relationship, or food binge. I found myself marrying my son's father" (Doyle, www.momastery.com).

Years later, Doyle embarked on an experiment. She decided to be a truth-teller in everyday life. No matter what happened, she decided she would be forthcoming with people. Rather than portray an image of herself as "all put together," as others saw her, she would let people see her true self and recount the experience in *Carry On, Warrior*.

One day, she writes, she was at the playground with another mother, Tess, and decided to simply speak the truth rather than keep it all inside. Doyle shared her personal story of being a recovering alcohol, drug and food addict, and how she accidently got pregnant and married the baby's father a year after they started dating. And how parenthood drove her to her wits' end, at times.

Tess was shocked by her response . . . yet also relieved.

Tess went on to confess that she was in a very difficult marriage, but felt she needed to act as though all were well, even though her life was absolutely not what it appeared. Doyle's truth-telling and vulnerability opened Tess up to be vulnerable as well. Their conversation at the playground was just the start of months of discussion between the two, which included building a support system for Tess and her family—connections with other like-minded, open, honest people who could help sort through their challenges. Doyle shares that over time, through hard work, vulnerability, and connection, Tess and her family became a healthy family again, and Doyle felt grateful to be a part of seeing how the truth set a family free (2013, 5).

❄❄❄

BOOB CANCER CHICK

Last year, I was co-facilitating a cancer support group for cancer patients at Saint Joseph Hospital in Denver. The group was new, so we often had only a few attendees. My co-facilitator, Melissa, and I were considering canceling the group after several months of low turnout. We wondered if it was serving much of a purpose. Then I received an email from one of the patients who had attended the group a few weeks prior. During the support group she shared that she was in a particularly dark place with her cancer diagnosis and not feeling very hopeful, even though her prognosis was relatively good.

She was stuck in the proverbial basement, unable to see her way to the balcony. She was scared and felt isolated and alone. When I shared my experience of my family loss and my own cancer fight—when I was vulnerable—the sharing had a positive impact on her. Below is the email I received from her. It made me laugh out loud.

> Hey—it's the boob cancer chick from the support group a few weeks ago. Just wanted to thank you for sharing your story with me. My anxiety was starting to affect my life and you helped me "take it down a notch." You're

making a big difference by sharing your story and being so positive. Happy Holidays!

Knowing that we'd made a difference in her life was hugely fulfilling for Melissa and me. We decided that even if we could only help *one* person, just like in the starfish parable, it was well worth it to keep the group going.

REFLECT

Write the following in your journal:

- Challenge yourself this week to share something about your life that displays some vulnerability. It could be something as simple as sharing with a friend that you had a hard day at work or had an argument with your partner; or perhaps it might be sharing with a colleague that you need help on a particular project.
- Each time you choose to share your vulnerability, journal about how it feels, and what the outcomes of that sharing are.

EPILOGUE

A BONUS CHOICE: GRATITUDE

"Gratitude is an immensely powerful force that we can use to expand our happiness, create loving relationships, and even improve our health."
—The Chopra Center

THINKING ABOUT WHAT WE are grateful for brings our physical and emotional hearts back to homeostasis within minutes, providing a sense of peace, equilibrium, and centeredness. It decreases the stress hormone cortisol in our bodies by over 20 percent and improves our mood and energy levels. Research by psychologists Robert Emmons and Michael McCullough found those who incorporate a grateful outlook into their daily lives noticed these changes:

- Felt better about their lives as a whole
- Experienced greater levels of joy and happiness

- Felt optimistic about the future
- Got sick less often
- Exercised more regularly
- Had more energy, enthusiasm, determination, and focus.
- Made greater progress toward achieving important personal goals
- Slept better and awoke feeling refreshed
- Felt stronger during trying times
- Enjoyed closer family ties
- Were more likely to help others and offer emotional support
- Experienced fewer symptoms of stress (2019)

Once I embraced faith, love, prayer, divine intervention, and vulnerability, I found myself feeling more and more gratitude for the challenges I had experienced. If I hadn't been faced with these challenges, I started to realize, I might still be that less mature version of myself who thought it was more important to *appear* centered than to actually *be* centered.

After Debbie's death, I became intricately involved with her boys, Brad and Adam—sixteen and fourteen years respectively when she passed; today they are thirty-three and thirty-one. I love them as if they were my own and have *immense* gratitude that they are part of our family. Harry, Luke, and Jake consider them brothers rather than cousins. Thankfully, Brad and Adam remember Debbie so well and have such fond memories of her. And they have her loving, compassionate spirit; her spirit is in them. They are *her*. Both Brad and Adam refer to me as their "second mom" and have expressed their gratitude for me loving them as much as I do and being there for them throughout the years—sentiments that warm my heart each and every day. When they both asked me to officiate their weddings, I couldn't hold back the tears of joy, honor, and gratitude. I know Debbie's spirit is joyful that we have the relationship we do; she wouldn't have wanted it any other way.

Today I am quite emotional when expressing the gratitude that I have in my heart to those I love. I am openly tearful with Brad and Adam and their spouses, Katie and Ali; our boys; my stepdaughters, Rachel and Tess; my family; friends; and Mark about how much love I have for them in my heart. I know I am truly blessed to be here with them on this earth. I think about it *daily*.

This sense of being true to my feelings, loving others with a full heart, not a heavy or fearful one, drives me each day and gives me purpose. I am much more authentic in my relationships. I tell people how much they mean to me. I *fear less* and *love more*, listen with greater intent, smile at strangers, and use names when communicating with those who wear name tags and badges—they feel noticed, and the smiles and energy that I typically get in return are always heartwarming. When helping others in need or volunteering in our community, I experience great joy and a sense of purpose; the giving and receiving is most certainly a two-way street. And every time I have a clean cancer scan, I feel I have a new lease on life and recommit to living a life full of love and connection.

Thank you for the opportunity to share my story through these pages. It has been a long, spiritual journey and a cathartic experience for me. I feel immense gratitude in my heart to be living each day. I never thought I would say that my cancer experience was a true blessing, but it was.

I hope you, too, can choose faith, love, prayer, divine intervention, and vulnerability to survive and thrive through your fears and unexpected challenges—to live a life full of joy, purpose, and fulfillment. Fear less, love more, and *make* it a great life.

REFLECT

Here are a few gratitude practices to try:

- Every day record in your journal one new thing that you are grateful for.
- Three times a year, send a handwritten thank-you note to someone who has had a significant impact on your life.
- Take a gratitude walk once a week: Notice the beauty around you—the sky, the trees, the birds, the flowers. Take it all in with deep breaths and center yourself, being grateful for all that surrounds you.

Marrying Brad and Katie in South Berwick, Maine,
September 29, 2018

One of my favorite pictures of Adam and Ali in Kittery,
Maine, after marrying them on August 22, 2020.

❊❊❊

Below are ten of my favorite quotes from the Fourteenth Dalai
Lama. I think they are all insightful and inspiring. I encourage
you to choose one quote that resonates, write it down, and put it
somewhere visible. May it be a good reminder of how you want
to show up in the world each and every day.

"Love is the absence of judgment."

"There is a saying in Tibetan, 'Tragedy should be
utilized as a source of strength.'
No matter what sort of difficulties, how painful
experience is, if we lose our hope, that's our real
disaster."

"Love and compassion are necessities, not luxuries.
Without them, humanity cannot survive."

"We don't need more money, we don't need greater
success or fame, we don't need the perfect body
or even the perfect mate. Right now, at this very
moment, we have a mind, which is all the basic
equipment we need to achieve complete happiness."

"Our prime purpose in this life is to help others. And
if you can't help them, at least don't hurt them."

"If you think you are too small to make a difference,
try sleeping with a mosquito."

"The creatures that inhabit this earth—be they human
beings or animals—are here to contribute to the
beauty and prosperity of the world. The food we eat,
the clothes we wear, have not just dropped from the
sky. This is why we should be grateful to all our fellow
creatures."

"For a person who cherishes compassion and love,
the practice of tolerance is essential, and for that, an
enemy is indispensable. So, we should be grateful

to our enemies, for it is they who can best help us
develop a tranquil mind."

"Old friends pass away, new friends appear. It is just
like the days. An old day passes, a new day arrives.
The important thing is to make it meaningful: a
meaningful friend—or a meaningful day."

"Remember that sometimes not getting what you
want is a wonderful stroke of luck."

ACKNOWLEDGMENTS

Thank you to all of you who made this book possible—my family, friends, colleagues, former clients, and soul groupers. A special thanks to all of you who shared your stories with me and graciously opened yourselves up to contribute your life experiences to this book. It meant a great deal to me and, I can only hope, to the readership.

A special thank-you to Koehler Books—all you need is one—and my editor Hannah Woodlan, for your editing expertise and encouragement. And to my dear friend Kristen Barletta, my former roommate at Boston College and editor and marketer extraordinaire.

Saving my immediate family for last, a heartfelt thank-you to Mark, Harry, Luke, and Jake, who generously shared their time with me over the years so I could tell this story. And to Rachel, Chris, Estelle, and Willa; Tess; Brad, Katie, and Lachlan; Adam and Ali—my family completes me. Love you to the moon and stars and back.

BIBLIOGRAPHY

Alexander, Eben, *Proof of Heaven: A neurosurgeon's journey into the afterlife*. New York: Simon & Schuster Paperbacks, 2012.

Bradberry, Travis, "5 Choices You'll Regret Forever." TalentSmart. 2015. Accessed April 1, 2020. https://www.talentsmart.com/articles/5-Choices-You'll-Regret-Forever-1705129096-p-1.html.

Brown, Adolph. www.docspeaks.com.

Brown, Brené, "The Power of Vulnerability." Ted.com. June 2010. https://www.ted.com/talks/brene_brown_the_power_of_vulnerability.

Chopra, Deepak, "Only A Silent Mind Can Be A Healing Mind." Chopra. March 30, 2020. https://chopra.com/articles/only-a-silent-mind-can-be-a-healing-mind.

Darwin, Charles, *Descent of Man*. London: Penguin Classics, 2004.

Doyle, Glennon. *Carry On, Warrior: The power of embracing your messy, beautiful life*. New York: Scribner, 2013.

Doyle, Glennon. www.momastery.com.

Doyle, Glennon, *Untamed*. New York: The Dial Press, 2020.

Eiseley, Loren, *The Unexpected Universe*. New York: Harcourt, Brace and World, 1969.

Emmons, Robert and Michael McCullough, "Cultivate the Healing Power of Gratitude," Chopra. November 3, 2012. https://www.chopra.com/articles/cultivate-the-healing-power-of-gratitude.

Groeschel, Craig, *Weird: Because Normal Isn't Working*. Grand Rapids: Zondervan, 2011.

Gunner, Caleb LP, "26 Things That Are Completely Under Your Control," #LIFEHACKS. Accessed April 1, 2020. https://lifehacks.io/things-you-can-control/.

Jammer, Max, *Einstein and Religion: Physics and Theology*. Princeton: Princeton University Press, 2002.

Lama, Dalai, Desmond Tutu, and Douglas Abrams, *The Book of Joy: Lasting happiness in a changing world*. New York: Avery, 2016.

Lamott, Anne, *Help, Thanks, Wow: The Three Essential Prayers*. New York: Penguin Group, 2012.

LaMotte, Sandee, "Being happier will help you live longer, so learn how to be happier." CNN Online. 2019. https://www.cnn.com/2019/09/03/health/happiness-live-longer-wellness/index.html.

Lewis, Clive Staples, *The Efficacy of Prayer*. 1958.

McCraty, Rollin, "Science of the Heart: Exploring the role of the heart in human performance: An overview of research conducted by the HeartMath Institute." HeartMath Institute. 2015. Accessed April 1, 2020. https://www.heartmath.org/research/science-of-the-heart/.

McGonigal, Kelly, "How to make stress your friend." www.ted.com. June 2013. https://www.ted.com/talks/kelly_mcgonigal_how_to_make_stress_your_friend.

Mejia, Zameena, "3 actions this felon-turned-CEO took to turn his life around." CNBC Make It. June 27, 2017. https://www.cnbc.com/2017/06/27/3-actions-this-felon-turned-ceo-took-to-turn-his-life-around.html.

Mitnick, Danielle, Richard Heyman, and Amy Smith, "Changes in relationship satisfaction across the transition to parenthood." *Journal of Family Psychology*, 23 (2009): 848-852. doi:10.1037/a0017004.

Perel, Esther, *Mating in Captivity*. New York: HarperCollins, 2017.

Poincenot, Jeremy. www.jeremypoincenot.com

Sasson, Remez. www.successconsciousness.com. 2016.

Segal, Marshall, "Prayer for Beginners." desiringGod. April 27, 2016. https://www.desiringgod.org/articles/prayer-for-beginners.

Taylor, Steve, "The Power of Purpose: Why is a sense of purpose so essential for our well-being?" Psychology Today. July 21, 2013. https://www.psychologytoday.com/us/blog/out-the-darkness/201307/the-power-purpose.

Thomas, Raven. "7 Signs That Someone You've Met Someone

From Your Soul Group." 2016. Accessed April 1, 2020. https://mysticalraven.com.

Waldinger, Robert, "What makes a good life? Lessons from the longest study on happiness." TEDx.com. November 2015. https://www.ted.com/talks/robert_waldinger_what_makes_a_good_life_lessons_from_the_longest_study_on_happiness.

Walia, Arjun, "Nothing Is Solid & Everything Is Energy—Scientists Explain the World of Quantum Physics." Collective Evolution. September 27, 2014. https://www.collective-evolution.com/2014/09/27/this-is-the-world-of-quantum-physics-nothing-is-solid-and-everything-is-energy/.

Warren, Rick, *The Purpose Driven Life.* Grand Rapids: Zondervan, 2002.

Weaver, Jen, "How to pray: 5 steps for beginners." Jen Weaver. Accessed April 1, 2020. https://www.thejenweaver.com/how-to-pray-beginners.

Williamson, Marianne, *A Return to Love: Reflections on the Principles of a Course in Miracles.* New York, NY: HarperOne, 1992.

Witt, Keith, "How to deal with the inevitable relationship entropy." Elephant Journal. December 24, 2016. https://www.elephantjournal.com/2016/12/how-to-deal-with-the-inevitable-relationship-entropy/.